World of Science 1

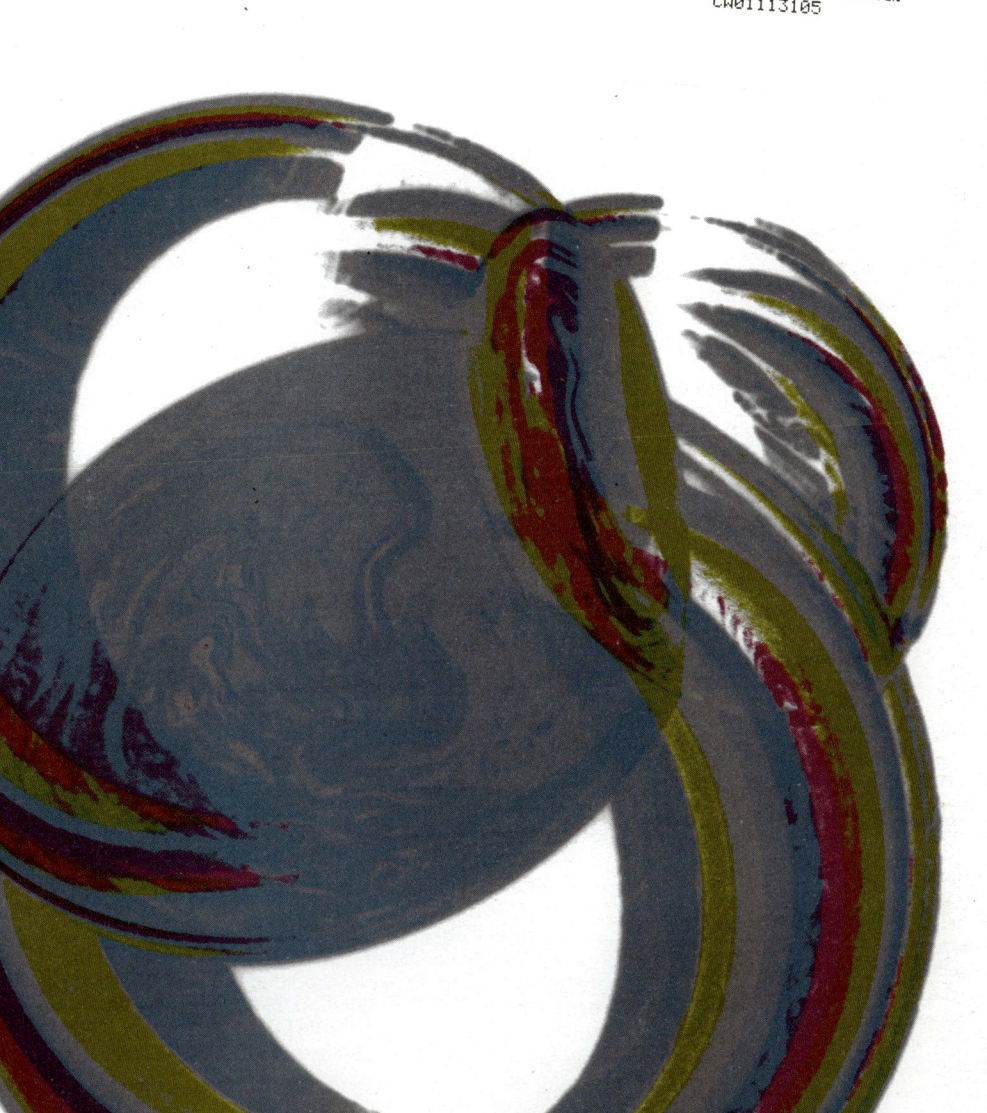

Graham Booth
Bob McDuell
John Sears

OXFORD
UNIVERSITY PRESS

Great Clarendon Street, Oxford OX2 6DP

Oxford University Press is a department of the University of Oxford. It furthers the University's objective of excellence in research, scholarship, and education by publishing worldwide in

Oxford New York

Athens Auckland Bangkok Bogotá
Buenos Aires Calcutta Cape Town Chennai
Dar es Salaam Delhi Florence Hong Kong
Istanbul Karachi Kuala Lumpur Madrid
Melbourne Mexico City Mumbai Nairobi
Paris São Paulo Singapore Taipei Tokyo
Toronto Warsaw

and associated companies in
Berlin Ibadan

Oxford is a registered trade mark of Oxford University Press

© Graham Booth, Bob McDuell, John Sears
The moral rights of the author have been asserted

First published 1999

All rights reserved. No part of this publication may be reproduced, stored in a retrieval system, or transmitted, in any form or by any means, without prior permission in writing from Oxford University Press. Within the UK, exceptions are allowed in respect of any fair dealing for the purpose of research or private study, or criticism or review, as permitted under the Copyright, Designs and Patents Act, 1988, or in the case of reprographic reproduction in accordance with the terms and licences issued by the Copyright Licensing Agency. Enquiries concerning reproduction outside these terms and in other countries should be sent to the Rights Department, Oxford University Press, at the address above.

This book is sold subject to the condition that it shall not, by way of trade or otherwise, be lent, re-sold, hired out or otherwise circulated without the publisher's prior consent in any form of binding or cover other than that in which it is published and without a similar condition including this condition being imposed on the subsequent purchaser.

British Library Cataloguing in Publication Data
Data available

ISBN 0 19 914697 7

Printed by Conti-Tipocolor s.r.l., Italy.

Acknowledgments
The publisher would to thank the following for their kind permission to reproduce the following photographs:

p 8 Oxford Scientific Films/P O'Toole (centre), Science Photo Library/A & H Frieder Michler (right), SPL/C Nuridsany (left), SPL/P McZell (bottom left), p 9 OSF/G Bernard (left), OSF/J Cooke (centre), OSF/D Dennis (centre right), SPL/J Revy (top right & centre), p 10 Heather Angel p 10 SPL/Eye of Science (centre & right), p 11 SPL/V Steger (top right), Science & Society Picture Library (left), SPL/A & H Frieder Michler (centre), p 13 SPL/A Pasieka, SPL/A & H Frieder (left), SPL/C Nuridsay & M Perennou (centre), p 14 SPL/J Durham (top), SPL/A & H Frieder Michler (centre), SPL/Dr J Burgess (bottom), p 15 SPL/M Kage, SPL/A Syred, SPL/Biophoto Photos (left), p 16 SPL/C Nuridsay & M Perennou, p 17 SPL/B Iverson, p 18 SPL/G Cox, SPL/Biophoto Associates (centre), OSF/Carolina Biological Supply Co (bottom), p 22 SPL/B Lehnhausen (left), p 25 J Allan Cash, p 27 Dr A Waltham (right), GeoScience Features (left & centre), p 30 SPL/Biophoto Associates, p 32 J Allan Cash (top), OSF/S Turner (centre), pp 34 SPL (left & right), 35, 41, p 42 SPL/R Hansen (left), SPL/S Terry (right), p 53 SPL/PMenzel (right), p 54 J Allan Cash (right & centre right), p 54 OSF/G Bryce (bottom left), p 57 OSF/L Crowhurst (bottom), OSF/H Fox (bottom right), SPL/V Fleming (bottom left), OSF/Partridge Films (top right), OSF/A Walsh (centre right), p 58 OSF (top), Heather Angel (left), OSF/S Dattari (bottom), p 59 OSF/J Cooke (top), OSF/B Herrod (right), OSF/G Bernard (bottom), p 60 Heather Angel (top), OSF/Z Leszcynski (centre), OSF/M Gibbs, p 61 SPL, p 64 Dr A Waltham (left & centre), SPL/F Sauze (right), p 70 J Allan Cash (top), SPL/A Sternberg (bottom), p 74 SPL/NASA, p 77 J Allan Cash, p 78 Allsport (bottom), p 84 J Allan Cash (top & centre), p 85 Mary Rose Trust, p 86 J Allan Cash (top), p 89 OSF/M Fogden (top), Heather Angel (centre), OSF/A Lister (bottom), p 91 OSF/S Dalton (top), OSF/M Hamblin (centre), p 93 SPL/Dr J Burgess (centre), SPL (bottom), OSF/G Maclean (bottom left), Heather Angel (bottom centre), OSF/H Taylor (bottom right), p 96 SPL/J Wlash, p 97 SPL/Biophoto Associates, p 97 D Schard, p 99 OSF/J Frazier (left), SPL/Petit Format/Nestle (centre & right), p 100 Dr A Waltham, SPL/C Winters, p 103 Science & Society Picture Library, p 104 SPL/D Nunuk, p 105 SPL/J Mead, p 106 J Allan Cash (left & centre), p 110 GeoScience Features (left), p 114 Boxmag Rapid.

Additional photography by Peter Gould

The Turtle from Candy is Dandy: *The Best of Ogden Nash* reproduced by permission of Andre Deutsch Ltd.

All efforts have been made to acknowledge copyright of material. If there are any omissions please contact the Publisher at the address above.

The publishers would like to thank:Sallie Hanlon, Banbury School; Trevor Hook, Clere School; Martin Rees, Cooper School for their help with World of Science

The illustrations are by:
John Paul Early, Jane Fern, David Graham, Nick Hawken, Ian Heard, Gillian Martin and Oxford Illustrators

Cover Photographs: Pete Turner/Image Bank

Introduction: Being a scientist

You will have a good idea of what science is from topics you have covered in primary school. You will study science throughout your secondary school. You may know that science can be split into a number of subjects:

- **biology** is the study of living things, whether plants or animals
- **chemistry** is the study of matter and the way that changes or reactions can occur
- **physics** is the study of how matter behaves and the relationships between matter and energy.

There are other sciences including astronomy, geology, and meteorology. Your science course for Years 7-9 will cover all of these sciences in a broad and balanced way. In Years 10 and 11 you may continue to study science either as one subject or as a number of separate subjects.

Practical science

In your primary school you will have done some practical science. You will have planned experiments, carried them out, taken results and drawn conclusions. You will do more experiments and hopefully you will be able to apply good scientific methods to problems. These problems may be ones you have thought of or ones other people suggest to you.

The world of science

You are moving into a scientific world. You will continue to hear of new discoveries, inventions, and technologies; about genes, isotopes and microelectronics. Everybody needs to know the words scientists use. They need to have some understanding of important scientific issues, for example: the best use of energy resources, the effect of exhaust fumes on the environment, and the peaceful use of radioactivity.

Many people work in science or subjects that rely heavily on science and technology. You could well earn your living as a scientist. It is said that there are more scientists working today than ever before. It is certain in years to come science will continue to be a very important aspect of our lives.

We hope, as you use these books, you will learn the basic science you will need, and, more importantly, become enthusiastic about science.

Graham Booth
Bob McDuell
John Sears

Teacher's notes:
Chapter sections

Chapter sub-sections are denoted by line separators. Further details are given in the Teacher's Guide.

Questions at three levels

▲ = *answerable from the page*

● = *needs some student interaction*

■ = *requires student interaction*

Contents

How to be a scientist (1)   6
How to be a scientist (2)   7

Life and living things

1.01 What is life?   8
1.02 Life processes   9
1.03 The meaning of life   10
1.04 Seeking out cells   11
      Finding out: Using a microscope   12
1.05 Common features of cells   13
1.06 Special features of cells   14
      Finding out: Investigating animal cells   15
      Finding out: Investigating plant cells   16
1.07 Specialized cells   17
1.08 Tissues and organs   18
1.09 Systems (1)   19
1.10 Systems (2)   20
1.11 Systems in mammals   21

Making mixtures

2.01 Melting and boiling   22
2.02 Evaporation   23
      Finding out: Heating water   24
2.03 Changes on cooling   25
2.04 Dissolving   26
2.05 Crystals   27
      Finding out: Crystals from a melt   28
      Finding out: Crystals from a solution   29
2.06 Colloids   30
2.07 Making a cake   31
2.08 Combustion   32
2.09 Mass changes on combustion   33
2.10 The discovery of oxygen   34
2.11 The theory of combustion   35
2.12 Acids, alkalis, indicators   36
      Finding out: Red cabbage as an indicator   37
2.13 Acid and alkali strength   38
2.14 Carbonates and acid   39
      Finding out: Heating substances   40
2.15 Physical and chemical changes   41

Electricity/charge

3.01 Electricity on the move   42
3.02 Circuits and symbols   43
3.03 Using switches   44
3.04 Measuring current   45
3.05 A series of things   46
3.06 Current in series circuits   47
      Finding out: Current in series circuits   48
3.07 In parallel   49
3.08 Current in parallel circuits   50
      Finding out: Current in parallel circuits   51
3.09 How bright?   52
3.10 Getting charged up   53

Variation, classification, and keys

4.01 Everyone is different   54
4.02 Vive la différence!   55
      Finding out: Looking at variation   56
4.03 Sorting out millions   57
4.04 Kingdoms of life   58
4.05 Plant body plans   59
4.06 Animal body plans   60
4.07 A biologist's solution   61
4.08 The key to life   62

Separating mixtures

- **5.01** Pure substances   63
- **5.02** Pure salt from rock salt   64
- Finding out: Purification of rock salt   65
- **5.03** Pure water from sea water   66
- **5.04** Further distillation   67
- **5.05** Mixing liquids   68
- **5.06** Separating ethanol and water   69
- **5.07** Uses of fractional distillation   70
- **5.08** Separating dyes   71
- **5.09** Chromatography   72
- Finding out: Orange squash dyes   73

Forces

- **6.01** Pushing and pulling   74
- **6.02** Getting going   75
- Finding out: Travelling downhill   76
- **6.03** Slowing down   77
- **6.04** Forces out of balance? (1)   78
- **6.05** Forces out of balance? (2)   79
- **6.06** The Earth's pull   80
- **6.07** Air can push   81
- Finding out: Falling down   82
- **6.08** Sinking   83
- **6.09** Floating   84
- **6.10** Raising a wreck   85
- **6.11** Forces that stretch   86
- Finding out: Springs   87
- **6.12** Using springs   88

Sex in plants and animals

- **7.01** The idea of reproduction   89
- **7.02** Sexy flowers   90
- Finding out: Flower structure   91
- **7.03** The go-betweens   92
- **7.04** Plants really do mate   93
- Finding out: Pollen and pollen tubes   94
- **7.05** The human life cycle   95
- **7.06** Human reproduction - male   96
- **7.07** Human reproduction - female   97
- **7.08** Menstrual cycle/fertilization   98
- **7.09** The baby grows   99

Metals

- **8.01** What is a metal?   100
- Finding out: Metals   101
- **8.02** Reactions of metals   102
- **8.03** Metals and non-metals   103
- **8.04** Metals and alloys   104
- **8.05** Corrosion of metals   105
- **8.06** Getting metals from rocks   106
- Finding out: Lead from lead oxide   107
- **8.07** Recycling metals   108

Magnetism

- **9.01** Magnets   109
- **9.02** A magnetic compass   110
- **9.03** Magnetic forces   111
- **9.04** Magnetic fields   112
- Finding out: Magnetic fields   113
- **9.05** Using magnets   114
- **9.06** Induced magnetism   115

INDEX   116

How to be a scientist (1)

Crash, bang, wallop!

Here is a disaster zone! But a real school science laboratory is one of the safest places in which to work. Good scientists always work carefully and safely. The Rules of the Laboratory have been forgotten by this class!

1 Look carefully at the *disaster zone* above.

  a Make a list of as many of the dangers as you can

  b From this list make up a set of **Rules of the Laboratory**

2 Make a rough sketch of the laboratory you normally use. Mark on it where the following items are usually kept:

  a bags and coats

  b Bunsen burners

  c beakers and other kinds of glassware

  d clamps and retort stands

  e power packs

  f metre rules

3 Very often safety rules in the laboratory are written negatively and start with *Don't do this, Don't do that, You should NOT …*

Rewrite your **Rules of the Laboratory** positively by starting with *Do this, Always, You should …*

Leave some space at the end of your list so you can add some more later. Stick the list in your exercise book.

How to be a scientist (2)

Making marvellous measurements!

How much pocket money do you receive? Whatever amount it is you'll want to know that you receive the right amount. If you receive more you might not complain, but what do you do if you receive less? Counting, or making a measurement of your pocket money is one measurement you make very carefully! And in the right units too!

Did You Know

One millilitre (1 ml) has the same volume as one cubic centimetre (1 cm^3), and one litre (1l) = 1000 cubic centimetres (1000 cm^3).

Making some measurements

	Length	Temperature	Time
Measuring device	ruler metre rule tape measure	thermometer	stopwatch stop clock
Units used	kilometre (km) metre (m) centimetre (cm)	degrees celsius (°C)	hour (h) minute (min) second (s)

	Mass	Volume of a solid	Volume of a liquid
Measuring device	balance electronic balance scales	measuring cylinder volume = 10 cm^3 of solid	measuring cylinder
Units used	tonne (t) kilogram (kg) gram (g)	cubic metre (m^3) cubic centimetre (cm^3)	litre (l) millilitre (ml) cubic centimetre (cm^3)

1. Which units are used to measure:
   a length   b time   c mass
2. When would you use:
   a a thermometer
   b a set of scales
   c a stopwatch
   d a measuring cylinder
3. Which measuring device and which unit would you use to measure the following:
   a the mass of a sack of coal
   b a mass of a bag of flour
   c the length of a garden
   d the volume of a large pebble
4. What units would be most sensible to use to measure the following:
   a a small bag of sweets
   b a small carton of orange drink
   c a carton of milk
   d the length of a car
5. Make a list of five measuring devices in your home.

7

CHAPTER 1

1.01

LIFE AND LIVING THINGS

What is life?

Imagine you are on the Starship Enterprise! You are boldly going to a new planet to seek out new life forms. On all these sorts of programmes the crew never have a problem telling if something has 'life signs'. How do they do it? What is it that tells them something is alive?

It is often true that if something moves it is alive, but what about a stream? Does the fact that water runs along make it alive? A car moves on a road, is it alive?

The preying mantis moves of its own accord

How can you tell if this plant is alive?

Flames move in the wind, are they alive?

Active or passive movement

The people on the starship have to have ways of telling active movement from passive movement. Perhaps they could use these definitions: Active movement is when a 'thing' moves itself: Passive movement is when something else makes it move. What about grass? You know this is alive and although bits of it can move, you cannot see this movement without looking inside the cells.

Living things are a very special group of 'things' in the natural world. They take non-living material and make it part of the living world. Living things then die and leave dead material behind. So when you look at the world you can divide the material in it into three groups; never lived, living, and dead.

A volcano creates new rock when the lava cools

1. All materials in the world can be divided into three groups. What are they?
2. Look at the pictures on this page. Decide which group each 'thing' in the picture fits into.
3. What is the difference between active and passive movement?
4. What other signs of life might there be?

Life processes

1.02

It is not easy to tell if something is alive just by looking at it. Think about a moss, a limpet or a mushroom. You 'know' they are alive, but apart from being told this, how do you know?

All living things must be able to do certain things. Living things are in fact defined by what they do. They are energy-using systems. Sometimes this involves processes we can see, like movement; more often the processes are not obvious to the naked eye.

The seven main processes of life

Probably the most obvious process is **reproduction.** All living things make more of their own kind. **Movement** is another process already mentioned. All living things move to some extent. Sometimes this will only be seen through a microscope; at other times the whole organism will move about. All living things take in food and water and other chemicals in order to make new parts. Taking in these things is called **nutrition.** Having taken some things in, all living things also get rid of wastes they do not want. This is called **excretion.**

Greenfly produce many young at once    Growth: from tiny seedling to mature plant

This mimosa plant is sensitive to touch (top = before; below = after)

Growth is another process that is easy to see in many life forms. Growth is the process of making new, or replacement, parts of the body and usually involves getting bigger. It is also important that living things can sense the world around them. This helps them find food and avoid danger. This ability to respond is called **sensitivity.**

All life needs energy to run these processes. The main way living things release energy is called **respiration.** Respiration is a way of getting energy out of food chemicals.

1. What are the seven processes of life?
2. One way of remembering the seven processes is to use the first letters of each word to jog your memory. For instance MRS GREN could be your very alive person! You could also make a phrase like Really Round Sheep Eat New Mown Grass. Make up your own memory jogger using the letters.
3. If you breathe in you get bigger, but you have not grown. How is breathing in different from growth?
4. Living things can be thought of as energy transformers. Explain why.

9

1.03 The meaning of life

Is there any sense in which crystals are alive?

How can you decide what is alive?

If life is a set of active processes (an energy-transforming system), how many of these processes do you need to have to be alive?

Suppose you had a very concentrated solution of salt. If one crystal forms, the whole solution will crystallize (turn into crystals). Is this reproduction? Is it growth? Is it enough to have only one of the processes to be alive?

Is a car alive? It burns fuel to get the energy out. This is very like respiration. It gives out the waste gas carbon monoxide among others. A car also feeds, moves and is sensitive, (but only when it has a driver with it). It never reproduces or grows.

There are two extra features of life that seem to be universal:
- all living things contain a blueprint made of **nucleic acid** (DNA or RNA).
- all living things are made from **cells**.

This would seem a very easy way of sorting out which things are alive.

The strange case of the virus

You will have heard of viruses and bacteria. Viruses may have made you ill. Colds and flu are caused by viruses. Bacteria may have made you ill. Food poisoning and German measles are caused by bacteria.

You might think that viruses and bacteria are alike. They are not. A bacterium is a cell that shows *all seven features of life*. It contains nucleic acid. A virus is just a 'box' made from protein. It contains nucleic acid too. But, unlike a bacterium, a virus does not respire, grow, feed, excrete, respond, or move. It takes over your cells and makes them produce more viruses – it reproduces!

Some scientists argue that because a virus contains nucleic acid and can reproduce, that it is alive.

Did You Know

You will have been infected many times by viruses! How many times have you had a cold or influenza. They are both caused by viruses. Other viruses include smallpox, polio, rabies, HIV, and AIDS.

Antibiotics and Viruses

Antibiotics are completely ineffective against viruses!

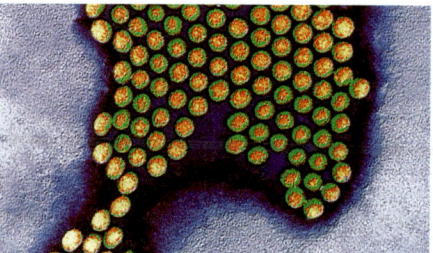
These viruses cause polio

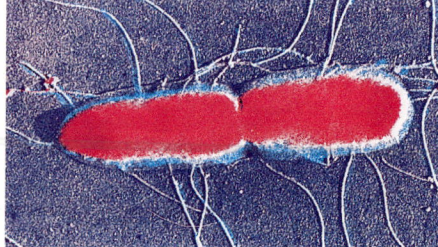
This bacterium causes typhoid

1. Explain why fire is not alive.
2. Explain clearly why crystallizing is not evidence of life and a virus reproducing is.
3. If you really were going to another planet, you would not necessarily expect life to have DNA. What would you include instead in your list of life-signs?

Seeking out cells

1.04

All living things work in the same basic way. They all feed, grow and excrete. They all respire, move and respond. They all reproduce. If these are the processes of life where do they take place? What we know owes a great deal to the invention of the microscope.

Simple microscope

People knew that lenses could be used to magnify things. You may have used a magnifying glass to make things look bigger. In 1676 a Dutchman, called Antonie van Leeuwenhoek, made a **simple microscope** which had one lens. He looked at rainwater and saw a lot of small organisms which he called animalcules.

Leeuwenhoek's microscope had a glass bead lens

Compound microscopes

Robert Hooke (1635–1703) was also one of the first to look at living things in this way. He used a **compound microscope**. This uses several lenses to magnify what you look at. Hooke looked at thin slices of cork. This is a material made by plants. What he saw were small, box-shaped objects which he called **cells**. It took another hundred and fifty years for scientists to be sure that all plants and animals are made of cells.

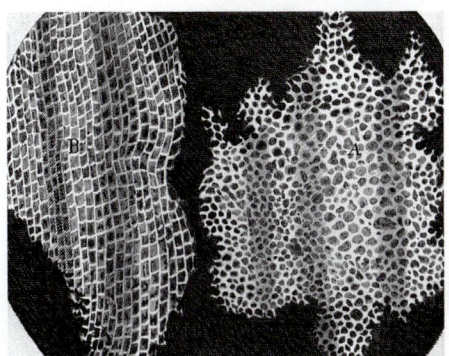
A slice of cork drawn by Robert Hooke – he invented the term cells

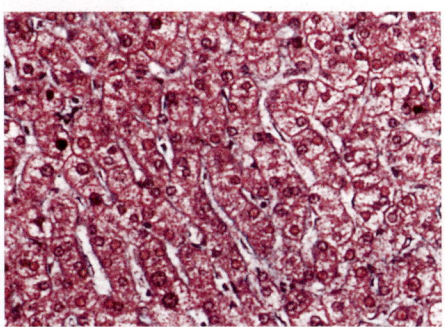
This is what you see when you look at liver cells with a light microscope. The stain makes it easier to see the cells' structure.

Convince Me

How would you go about convincing someone that plants and animals are made of cells?

To look at cells with a light microscope people use very thin layers of material. This lets light through the cells so that they can be seen. It is also a help to stain the cells. Some chemicals stain different parts of cells different colours. This helps show what is inside cells.

1. What is the difference between a simple and a compound microscope?
2. Why can you only study thin material in a light microscope?
3. Why do people use stains when studying cells?
4. Why do you think it took so long for people to be sure all plants and animals are made from cells.

Finding out: Using a microscope

Cells are so small that you need to magnify them to see them clearly. This means using a microscope.

The microscope has two sets of magnifying lenses. The one you look through is the **eyepiece lens**. The one nearest the object is the **objective lens**. Most microscopes have three objective lenses on a rotating disc. The lenses are different strengths.

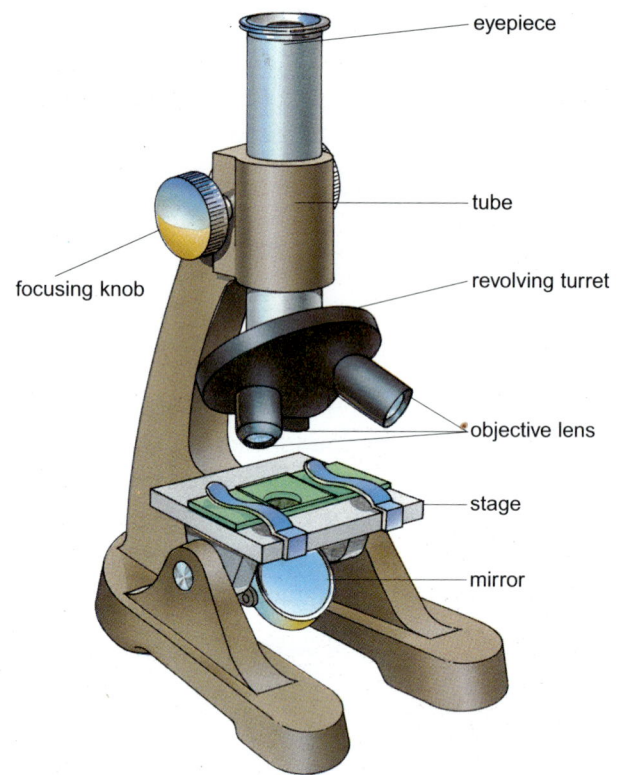

How to set up a microscope

1 Line up the shortest objective lens with the eyepiece.

2 Make sure it is clicked into place.

3 Use the large focus knob to move the tube down as far as it will go. There should be an automatic stop to prevent the lens hitting the stage.

4 If you have a mirror you should angle the flat side towards the light. If possible use daylight, **but do not point the mirror directly at the sun**. If you have a built in light turn it on.

5 Look through the eyepiece until you see an evenly lit field of view (a circle).

6 Adjust the diaphragm. This is worked by a little lever below the stage. Take the eyepiece out and look down the tube. Move the lever until you can just see the edge of the diaphragm coming into view around the circle. Put the eyepiece back.

7 Now you are ready to use the microscope. Remember not to move the microscope if you are using daylight.

How big is the field of view?

1 On a piece of transparent plastic (a bit of an overhead transparency sheet is good) draw a single thin black line and mark it in millimetres.

2 Put this flat on the stage so that the line is across the centre of the hole.

3 Look down the microscope and slowly turn the large focus knob. This will lift the tube up. The line will come into focus.

4 How many millimetre marks are there across the field of view?

5 You are now ready to look at cells with your microscope.

Common features of cells

1.05

All plants and animals are made up of cells. Cells can be thought of as the building bricks of life. Every cell is a busy chemical factory. It has to build new structures and break down old ones. All cells have certain things in common.

Each plant or animal cell contains a **nucleus.** This is the control centre of the cell. It contains a blueprint for the cell made from a chemical called **DNA.**

All cells are surrounded by a thin layer called a **membrane**. This barrier controls the things that come in and out of the cell. It will only let some things in and not others.

The main part of the cell is a jelly-like liquid called the **cytoplasm.** It is here that most of the chemical reactions take place.

The pictures show these three main parts in animal and plant cells.

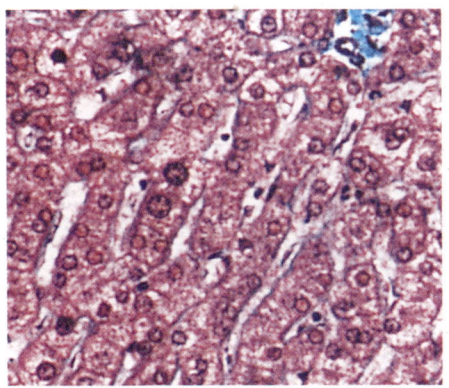
Typical animal cells (× 400)

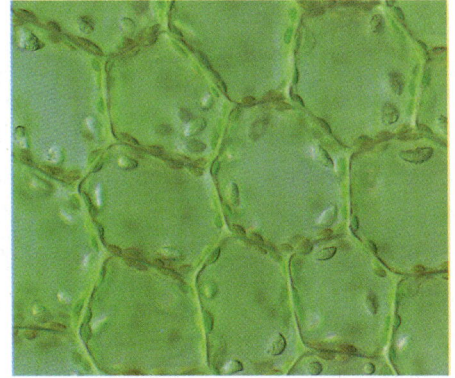
Typical plant cells (× 400)

Models help you imagine

It is hard to think about things as small as cells. Making models may help you to imagine them. You could think of the structure of the cell as a bag full of jelly with a smaller bag of jelly (the nucleus) inside it. Another way of thinking about cells is in terms of how they work. A cell is a bit like a building site. It has a main office (the nucleus) with the site plans inside (the DNA). It has a fence round it with controlled access only (the membrane). It has the main building area (the cytoplasm).

1. Name the three things found in all plant and animal cells.
2. Write down in your own words what each one does.
3. Find out what the letters DNA stand for.
4. Look at the scale on the picture of the plant cells. Work out how many cells you could fit along a line 1 cm long.

What Do You Think?

How big is an 'average' cell?

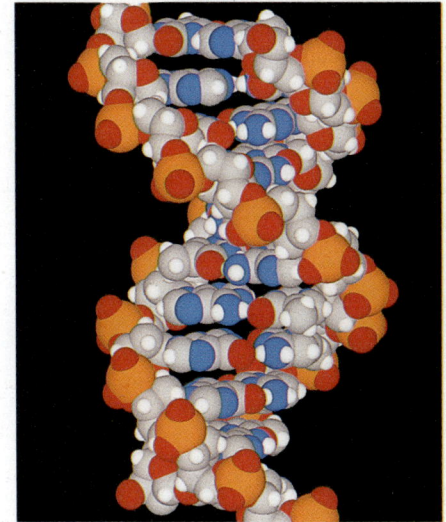
Plastic 'balls' are used to make an Atomic model of DNA

1.06 Special features of cells

Plants and animals have many things in common and their cells all have a nucleus, a membrane and cytoplasm. However, they live in very different ways. Plants stay still and make their own food, but animals eat ready-made food and usually need to move about to find it.

Differences between plant and animal cells

Plant cells have a **cell wall.** The wall is made of **cellulose** fibres woven together. There are plenty of gaps for chemicals to pass through so they can reach the cell membrane. You can think of this as a bit like the cardboard round a wine box. The bag of wine is the membrane and cytoplasm. The wall gives the plant cell a definite shape and size. All the cell walls together help to give the plant a firm structure so that it stays in position. Animal cells do not have cell walls.

Plant cells like the ones shown above on the left are also green. They have a green chemical called **chlorophyll** in the cells. It is held in special packets called **chloroplasts.** Chlorophyll uses the sun's energy so plants can make their own food. Animal cells do not have chloroplasts.

All cells have stores of liquid inside them. These are kept in special 'bags' called **vacuoles**. Useful chemicals, dissolved in water, are kept in the 'bags' until needed. Sometimes wastes are stored there until they can be removed. In plant cells there is one large vacuole. Animal cells usually have many small vacuoles.

Electron microscopes

Modern technology means that you can now look at cells with an **electron microscope**. Instead of shining light through cells, scientists use an electron beam. This makes a much greater magnification possible. This allows you to see very small structures, like chloroplasts, in detail.

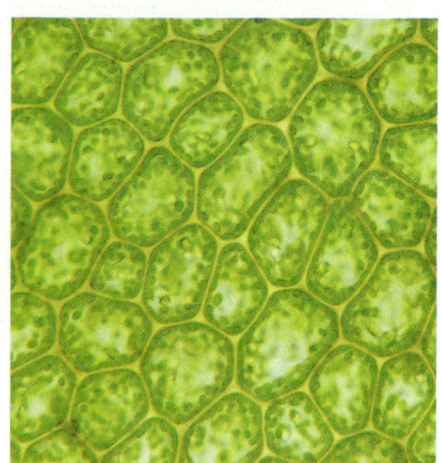

These plant cells (moss leaf) contain green chlorophyll in their chloroplasts

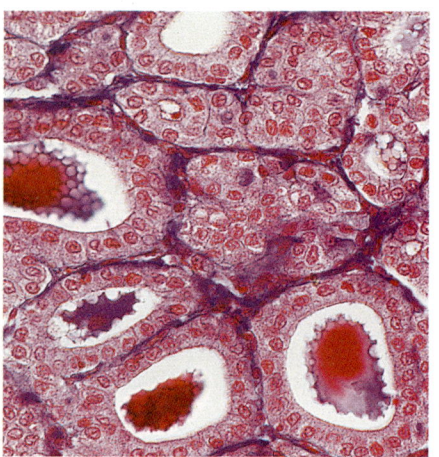

These secretory cells produce chemicals in their vacuoles

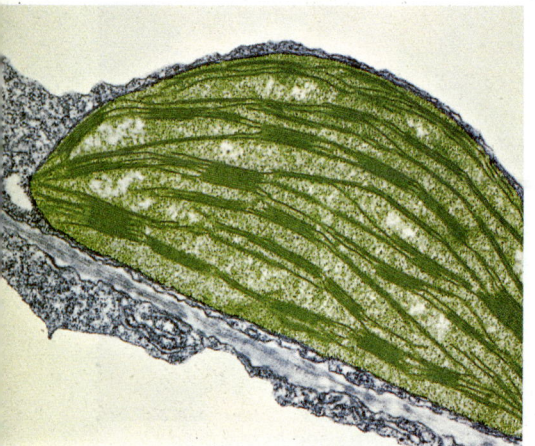

This electronmicrograph shows a chloroplast in great detail. The membranes hold chlorophyll in stacks

1. From the information in the text make a table of differences between plant and animal cells. Write your information in a table with two columns as shown.

Plant cells	Animal cells

2. Why would having cell walls make life difficult for animals?

3. To see things with an electron microscope you have to kill them and cut very, very thin slices which are then heavily stained. What problems might this create?

Finding out: Investigating animal cells

Instructions

1. Use a clean cotton bud to rub the inside of your cheek gently.
2. Rub the cotton bud onto the middle of a slide. Throw the cotton bud away. Do not use it again!

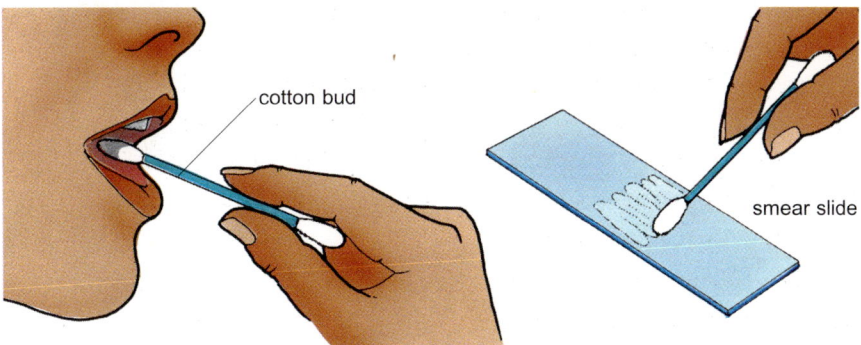

3. Put a drop of methylene blue on the middle of the slide.
4. Lower a cover slip over it.

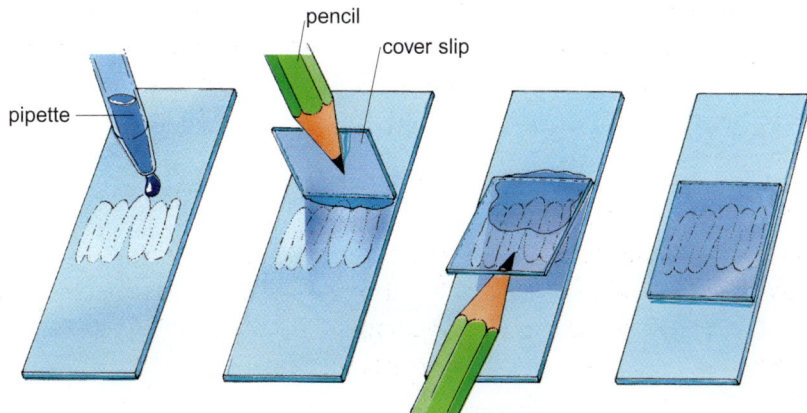

5. Look at the cells using your microscope. Remember to start with the lowest power objective lens and the tube right down. You should see cells like those in the photograph on the right.
6. Carefully draw what you see and label your drawing.

Note:
If you do not like to use your own cheek cells, you can look at dead skin cells instead. Put a small piece of Sellotape™ on your hand and then peel it off and stick it down to a slide. This will show you the size and shape of cells but you will not be able to see the contents.

WARNING

Methylene blue can stain.

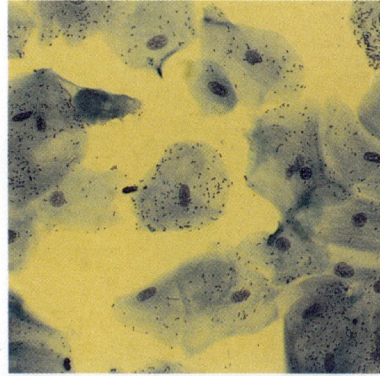

Cheek cells stained with methylene blue (x 1000)

Finding out: Investigating plant cells

WARNING

Glass cover slips can cut you if broken.

Iodine can stain.

Instructions

1. Peel away a strip of onion cells from the inner surface of a bulb layer.

½ onion   ¼ onion   one segment

2. Cut off a small (2 mm × 2 mm) piece and place it flat on your slide.

3. Put one drop of water near the edge of the onion strip.

4. Hold a cover slip by the drop so that the water runs along its edge.

5. Lower the cover slip gently using a pin or a pencil tip.

6. Set up your microscope and look at the strip on low power.

7. Turn the objective lens disc to the next highest power lens. You may need to refocus but only use the small focusing knob. You should see cells similar to those in the photograph.

8. Draw what you see and label your drawing.

9. To help you see the cells better make another slide using a drop of iodine solution instead of water. This stains the cells and makes the contents easier to see.

To see plant cells with chloroplasts you could look at moss leaves in the same way. They are one cell thick as well.

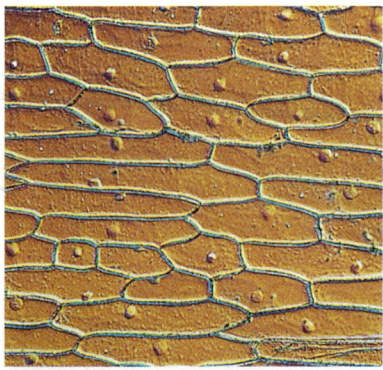

Onion cells stained with iodine (× 250)

16

Specialized cells

1.07

There are many different kinds of organisms. Some organisms are only made of one cell. These apparently simple creatures are called **protists.** They have to perform all the life processes in one cell (e.g. *Amoeba*). Some single-celled organisms are so small that they do not have all the internal structures of protists. These are **bacteria** which do not have a proper nucleus, although they do have DNA.

> **What do you think?**
> How small could a living thing get and still be alive?

Specialized cells

The most familiar organisms, however, like plants and animals, are made from many cells. This allows them to have specialized cells which only carry out a limited number of functions. This specialization means the cells can be better at doing a job than a general purpose cell would be. When you look at a specialist cell you should ask, 'How is its structure suited to what it does?' This is an example of a very important idea in biology, that of **adaptation.** You will return again and again to questions of how things are suited to the way they live.

Look at the ciliated epithelium cells in the picture. These cells line the inside of the windpipe. They act as a lining layer and are used to push the sticky mucus (blue), which is a dust trap, out of the lungs. You can see that they are regularly shaped and fit together neatly. They also have a layer of small 'hairs' (**cilia**) on the surface. These beat like oars in a boat to push the mucus along.

Now look at the picture of the root hairs of a plant. These hairs are part of the outer layer of the root. They are where water is taken into the plant. The hairs are part of the cells of the outer lining layer. They are regular with long projection. These grow out into the soil to come into contact with as much soil water as possible. This makes it easier for the plant to take in water.

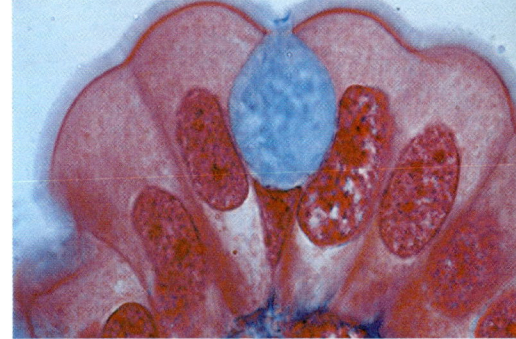
Ciliated epithelium (× 2500)

Root hair cells from marjoram (× 100)

---

1. What are the advantages of having many cells?

2. Try to explain how the gut cells shown opposite are adapted for absorbing food and giving out chemicals.

3. What might be the problems of having many cells?

4. Why would a plant cell in the dark not need chloroplasts?

5. Look at the specialist cells described in other sections of this book and explain how their structure is suited to their function e.g. eggs, sperm, and palisade cells

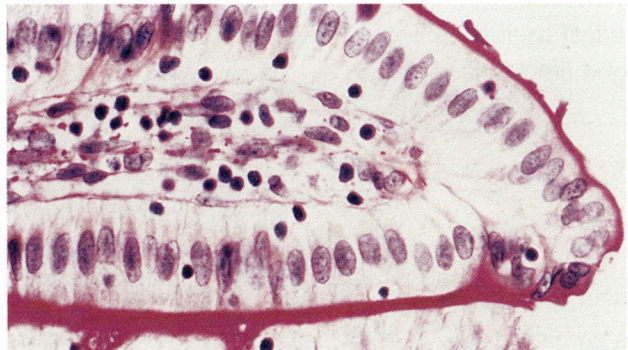
Lining cells from the gut of a mammal

1.08 Tissues and organs

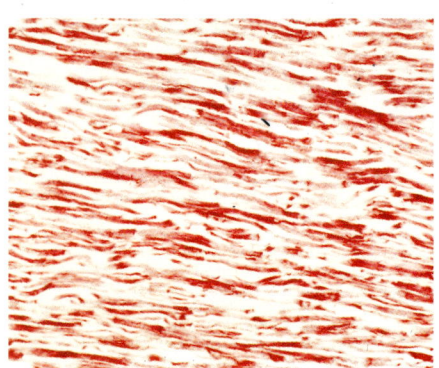
These cells work together to form a layer of connective tissue

Most living things have more than one cell. They are **multicellular**. Having many cells is so common there must be a good reason for it. One of the things it allows an organism to do is to specialize. If you only have one cell, then all the processes of life have to go on inside it. If an organism has many cells it can have different sorts of cell. These can specialize in particular jobs. Groups of specialist cells can work together to carry out a small number of jobs efficiently.

Tissues

A good example of specialist cells working together is muscle. A single muscle cell on its own could do very little. Groups of muscle cells working together can make an animal very strong or fast. Groups of cells working together are called **tissues**. The lining cells of your lungs also work together to form a thin protective tissue.

Organs

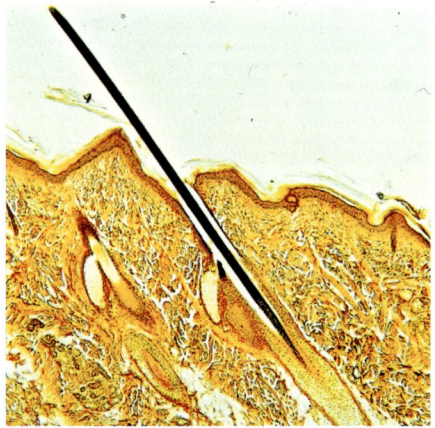
Skin is a complex organ

Groups of different cells are usually linked up with each other. Your skin is made up of a layer of very similar cells joined together to protect you from the knocks of everyday life, but it is not just made from lining cells. It also contains nerve endings, sweat glands and blood vessels. This means that skin is not just a tissue, although it contains tissues. It is an example of an **organ.**

Organs are groups of tissues working together for a particular function, or a set of related functions. For example, your skin works to detect and protect you from the outside world. Another example is your heart which works to pump blood around your body and although it is mainly muscle tissue there are other tissues in it as well (lining tissue, tendons and connective tissue for example).

Tissues and organs in plants

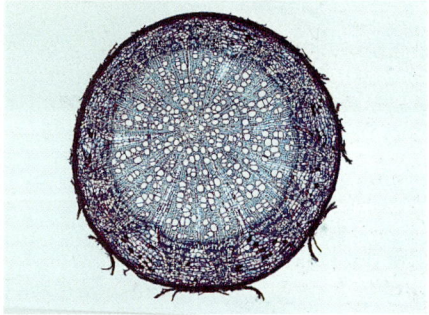
Cross-section of the root of a lime tree

Plants also have tissues and organs. The cells that carry water are one sort of tissue (**xylem**) and the cells that make most food in a leaf are another (**palisade** tissue). The leaf itself is an organ, made of several tissues. It is structured to make food efficiently.

1. What is a tissue?
2. What is an organ?
3. Why is it useful to have tissues and organs?
4. Find out what sort of tissues can be found in a root, a muscle, and an eye.

18

Systems (1)

1.09

The parts of an organism that carry out a particular life process form a **system** in the body. A system is made of a variety of organs working together. All organisms have the following seven systems:

- **reproductive** system
- **movement** system
- **nutritional** system (in animals this is the *digestive* system)
- **excretory** system
- **growth** system
- **responsive** system (sensitivity)
- **respiratory** system

Sometimes these systems are divided up further. For instance the movement system is made up of the skeletal system and the muscular system.

In the responsive system the main sense organs are found separately but are linked through the brain by the nerves of the nervous system.

Sometimes the organs in a system are not linked physically. For instance, the milk-producing (mammary) glands in mammals are not physically linked to the ovaries or womb. In this case chemicals enable the organs of the reproductive system to work together.

The digestive sytem

Look at the diagram of the digestive system. You can see that it is made up of the gut, the liver and gall bladder, and the pancreas. (The gut is made up of several specialized sections which are thought of as organs.) Each of these organs contains several tissues and they all work together to digest and absorb food. In this system all the organs are joined together physically.

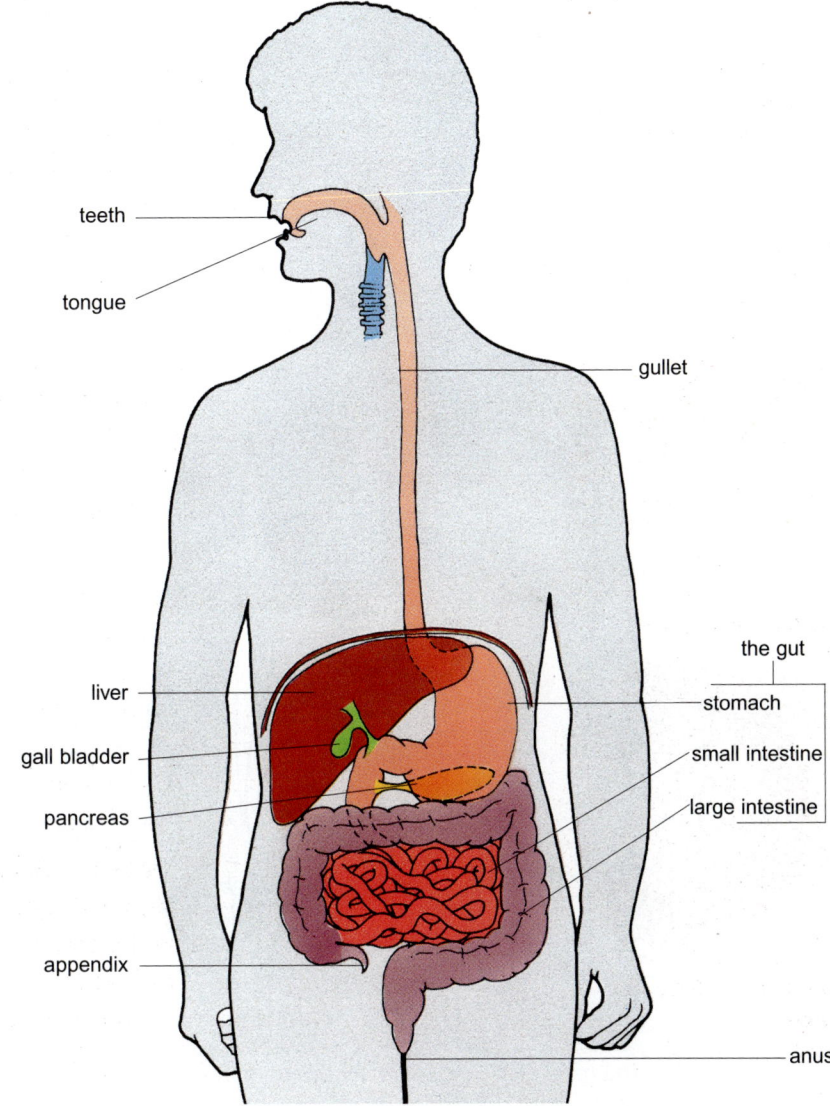

The digestive system (with organs shown for clarity)

1. What are the main organs in the digestive system?
2. The sensory system helps detect the world around us. Find out what the six main senses are and where the main organs of the system are.
3. Can you think of another system where some organs are physically separate from the others.

19

1.10 Systems (2)

The excretory system has two kidneys and a bladder. It works by filtering blood. In this way it is linked to the circulatory (transport) system. The transport system provides the links to all the other systems in multi-cellular organisms.

Special plant systems

Plants also have systems such as the support and transport systems. In the transport system tissues such as xylem and phloem work together to carry water and food throughout the plant. The movement of these materials also involves the stomata (holes) in the leaves and active pressure from the roots. In this way several parts of the plant work together to achieve the overall function.

All working together

All systems work together to make an organism. They all need to work at the right speed and time so that the organism keeps going. It is only when things go wrong in one system that we become aware of the importance of keeping everything coordinated!

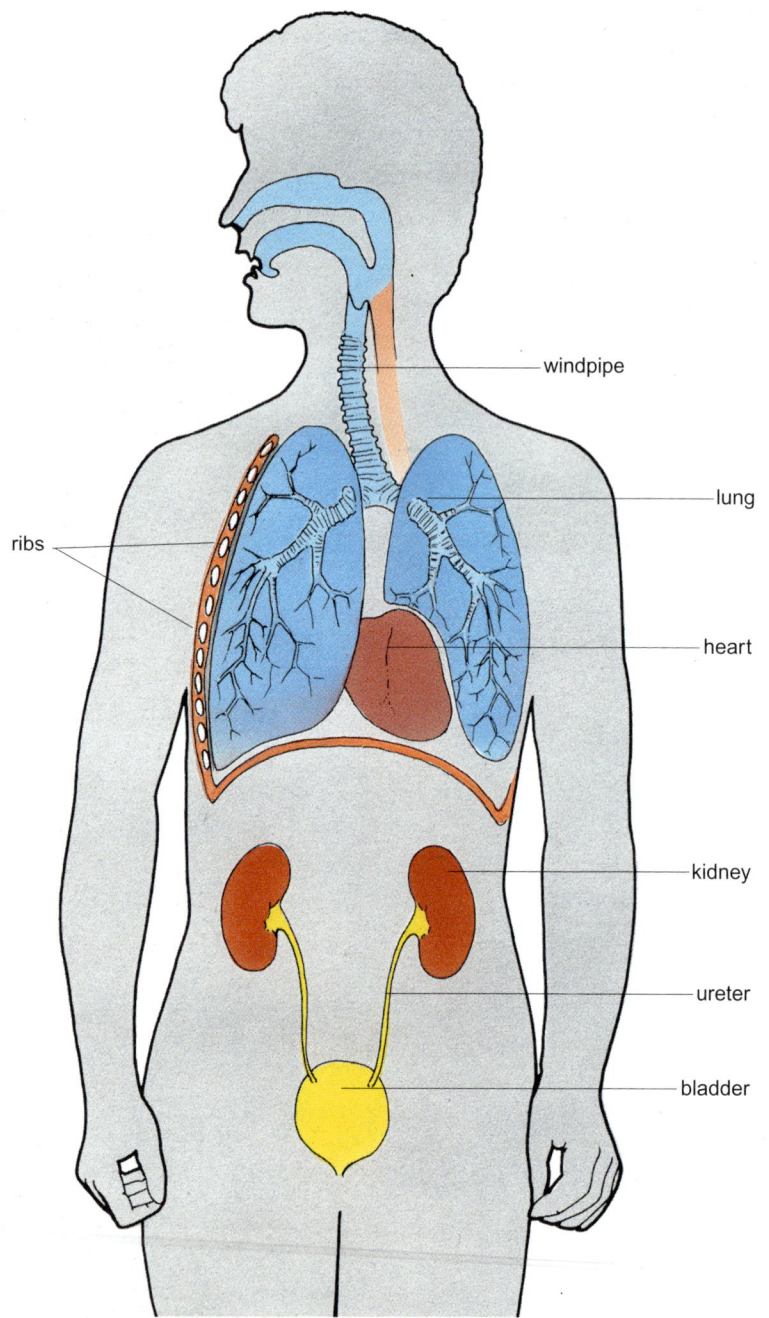

The respiratory and excretory systems

What Do You Think?

Is a system more than the sum of its parts?

 1 What are the main organs in the excretory system?

2 What are the main tissues and organs in plants that are involved in reproduction?

3 Could a group of organisms link to form a 'super organism'?

Systems in mammals

1.11

A good way to appreciate the structure of a whole organism is to look at the real thing. To see the inside structure of a whole animal you need to watch a dissection. The illustrations of a dissected Guinea pig show you how organs and systems are put together inside an animal.

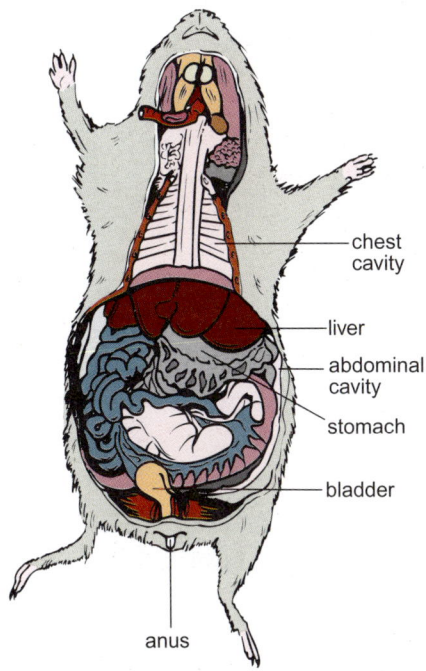

Inside the abdominal cavity: the main digestive organs

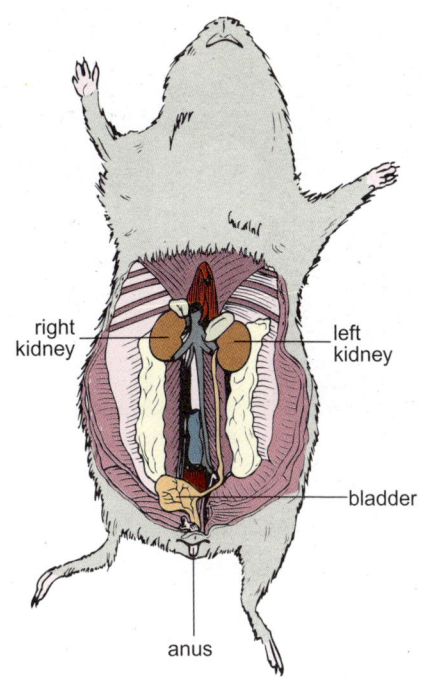

Further inside the abdominal cavity: the kidneys and bladder

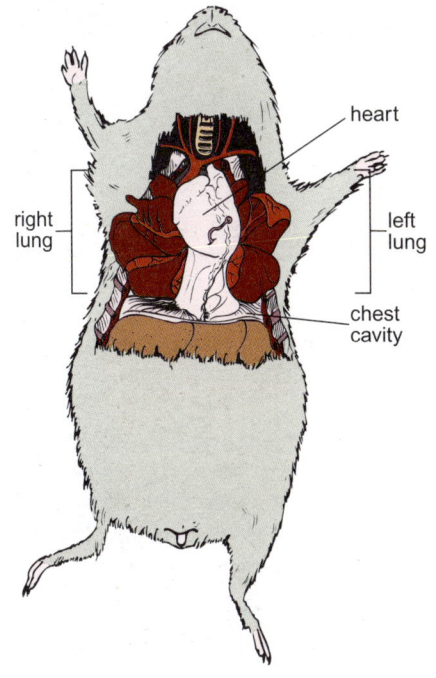

Inside the chest cavity: the lungs and heart

Ask Your Teacher!

You may also have models in your school that you can use to help you understand how the organs and systems fit together.

1. Where are the kidneys in relation to the gut?
2. Where is the heart in relation to the lungs?
3. Which system connects all the others together by carrying food and water to them?
4. Which system links all the others and co-ordinates their actions?

21

CHAPTER 2

2.01 MAKING CHANGES

Melting and boiling

Melting

Although the Sun is shining it will take a long time for the iceberg (left) to change to water. This change from solid to liquid is called **melting** (to a **molten** liquid). Two other examples of solids melting to form liquids are candle wax and an ice lolly. Melting takes place at the **melting point**.

Iceberg/floating ice

melting takes place here

Two examples of solids melting

Did You Know?

There are plans to tow two icebergs from the North Pole to hot countries that are short of drinking water. Icebergs melt only very slowly.

In 1912 a passenger ship on its first voyage from Great Britain to America was sunk when it collided with an iceberg. The ship was called the *Titanic*.

Boiling

When water is heated in a kettle, the temperature of the water rises. When the temperature reaches 100 °C the water **boils**. Liquid water changes into a **gas** or **vapour**. The temperature at which boiling takes place is called the **boiling point**. Different liquids have different boiling points.

Changes of state

Melting and boiling are called **changes of state**.

---

1 Copy and finish the following:

solid → liquid → gas

2 All materials can be in three different states – solid, liquid or gas. In which state are the following materials at room temperature?

  a polythene

  b petrol

  c air

  d limestone

3 Here are some melting and boiling points.

Material	Melting point/ °C	Boiling point/ °C
ethanol	−117	78
antifreeze	−16	198
oxygen	−218	−183
sulphur	113	444

  a Which material has the highest melting point?

  b Which material has the lowest boiling point?

  c In which state are each of the materials at room temperature? Room temperature is 20°C.

  d Which material is liquid over the largest range of temperature?

Evaporation

2.02

The first photograph shows a saucer filled with water. The second photograph shows the saucer one week later. All of the water has disappeared. During the week the water has **evaporated**. During **evaporation** water escapes from a liquid and goes into the air.

> **Did You Know?**
>
> Boiling and evaporation are both changes from liquid to gas or vapour. How are they different?

1. The saucer and the water (see above) were weighed at the start of the week. How would this weight change during the week?

2. The experiment in Q1 was repeated four more times (see i-iv below).
   a. What must be kept the same if it is to be a **fair test**?
   b. For each experiment, do you think the evaporation will be faster, slower, or the same as before?

3. Clothes may be dried in the garden on a washing line. The water on the clothes evaporates. What conditions make the clothes dry quickly?

4. If your teacher put a drop of methylated spirit on the back of your hand it would quickly evaporate. What would you feel when the liquid evaporated?

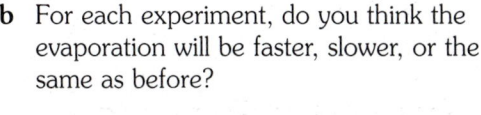

(ii) Using a tall glass instead of a saucer

(i) In a warmer room

(iii) With a fan blowing air over the surface of the water

(iv) With a thin layer of oil floating on the water

23

Finding out: Heating water

In this experiment you will heat crushed ice with a steady Bunsen burner flame and record the temperature at half minute intervals until the water is boiling.

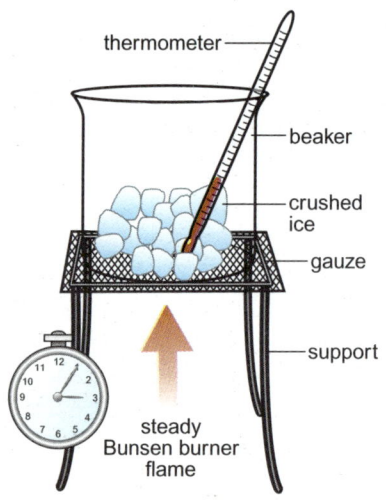

Instructions

1. Light the Bunsen burner and adjust until the flame is about 5 cm high and the airhole is half open. Do not adjust the Bunsen burner during the experiment as you need to make sure the amount of heat produced each minute is constant.

2. Move the Bunsen burner until it is underneath the support and gauze.

3. Half fill the beaker with crushed ice and stir with the thermometer. Record the temperature when it is constant.

4. Place the beaker on the support and start timing. Stir continuously and record the temperature every half minute. Try to do this without removing the thermometer from the water.

5. Continue heating and recording the temperature until the water is boiling steadily.

6. Copy and complete the following table. Make sure you have enough space on your page to include all your results.

Time/ min	Temperature/ °C
0	
1/2	
1 1/2	

WARNING

Leave the Bunsen burner, gauze, and support to cool before touching them.

7. Plot a graph of the temperature of the water against time. Draw your axes as shown in the diagram.

8. Give two reasons why the temperature rises slowly at the start of the experiment.

9. What is observed on the outside of the beaker in the early stages of the heating?

   Explain how this is formed.

10. At about 60 °C some bubbles of gas can be seen escaping.

    What are these bubbles and why are they formed?

Changes on cooling

2.03

The steamy bathroom
What happens to a mirror in the bathroom if you have a hot bath or shower, especially on a cold day? The mirror steams up so you can no longer see yourself. The water vapour or steam is turning to liquid water on the cold surface of the mirror. This is called **condensation** and the water vapour is **condensing** on the cold surface.

Making ice lollies
Have you ever made ice lollies by putting orange squash in a mould in the freezer? As the orange squash cools the liquid turns to a solid called **ice**. The liquid is said to **freeze.** This takes place at the **freezing point.** For pure water the freezing point is 0 °C but for orange squash it is slightly lower.

The ice lolly is different from the orange squash. It has a definite shape and it is hard.

Other liquids will freeze if you cool them to the correct temperature.

1. Name some other examples of condensation.
2. Copy and finish the following:

   gas or vapour → liquid → solid
   (with blanks above the arrows)

3. The picture shows tar being used to re-surface a road.

   Copy these sentences and finish them using words from the list.

   freeze   gas   liquid   melt   solid

   The tar is heated until it is _____ and then poured onto the road. On cooling the tar turns to a _____. On a very hot day the tar may _____ and form a liquid.

4. Why does water drip out of a car exhaust on a cold morning when a car engine is started?

25

2.04 Dissolving

Sugar in tea and coffee
Do you take sugar in tea or coffee? You can no longer see the sugar when you stir it because the sugar has dissolved. The sugar **dissolves** in the hot liquid.

The substance which is dissolved is called the **solute**. The substance in which the solute dissolves is called the **solvent**. The resulting mixture is called a **solution**.

Sam puts six spoonfuls of sugar in his tea. When he stirs it there is still sugar at the bottom of the mug. This is because a mug of hot tea can only dissolve a certain amount of sugar. If too much is used, the extra sinks to the bottom.

> **Did You Know?**
>
> Water is a very good solvent. It dissolves more substances than any other solvent. It is almost impossible to keep water pure because it will dissolve so many of the things it comes in contact with. There are many other solvents. Can you think of the names of any?

A solution which contains as much as can possibly be dissolved, at a given temperature, is called a **saturated solution**. The amount that will dissolve depends upon the amount of liquid and the temperature of the liquid.

A substance that dissolves is said to be **soluble**. A substance that does not dissolve is said to be **insoluble**.

---

1. In a cup of sweet tea or coffee how do you know the sugar is still there?

2. The table gives the number of small spoonfuls of sugar dissolving in a mug of tea at different temperatures.

	Temperature/ °C			
	20	40	70	90
number of spoonfuls of sugar dissolving	1	1½	2½	4

   What pattern can you see between the number of spoonfuls of sugar dissolving and the temperature of the tea?

3. What name is given to a solution which contains the maximum amount of dissolved solute at a particular temperature?

4. When salt is added to water the salt dissolves.
   What name is given to
   a the salt
   b the water
   c the mixture of salt and water?

26

Crystals

2.05

The photographs below show some crystals of different materials. If you look at crystals you will notice that they have regular shapes.

Crystals can be made by cooling a molten substance until the melt solidifies. This is the way that many crystalline rocks in the Earth were formed.

Another way of producing crystals is to let a hot, saturated solution cool. The diagram below shows how crystals of copper(II) sulphate can be made by cooling a hot, saturated solution of copper(II) sulphate.

> **Did You Know?**
> The word crystal comes from the Ancient Greek word for ice.

Making copper(II) sulphate crystals

The seven crystal shapes

Crystals only exist in seven different shapes. Because there are only seven possible structures, many substances have the same crystal shape. For example, both salt and sugar have cubic crystals. Substances with the same crystal shape are said to be **isomorphous**. This word means 'same shape' in Greek.

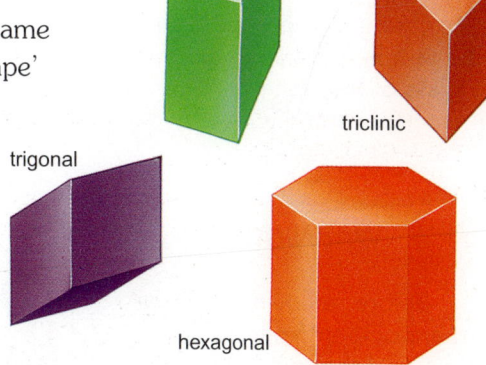

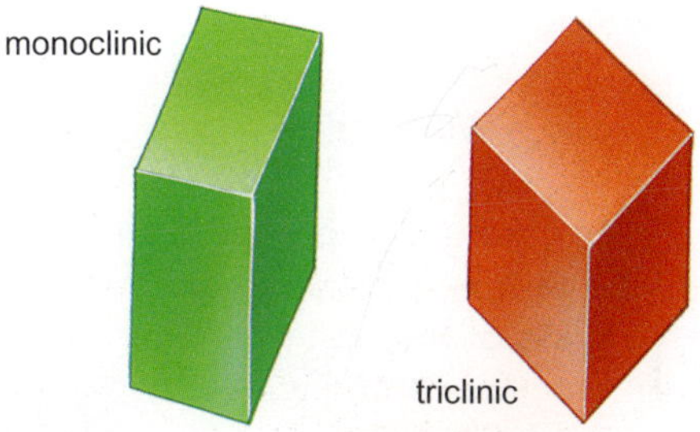

The seven possible crystal structures

1. A cubic crystal is like a dice. It has six faces. How many faces are there on each of the crystal shapes in this diagram?

2. Why do crystals form when a hot solution of copper(II) sulphate is cooled?

27

Finding out: Crystals from a melt

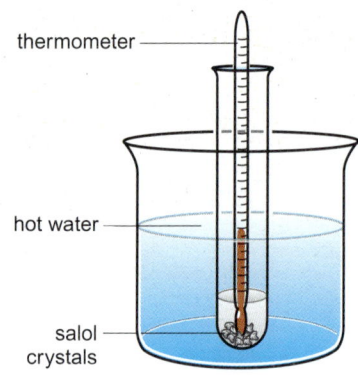

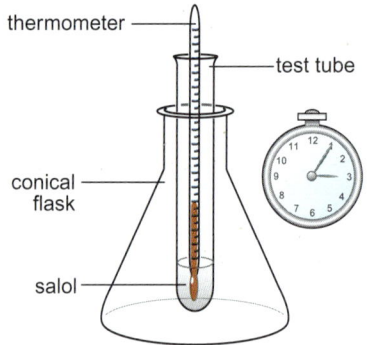

Salol is a substance with a low melting point. You are going to melt some salol and then allow it to cool until crystals are re-formed.

Instructions

1. Half-fill the beaker with hot water.
2. Put 4 cm depth of salol crystals into the test tube.
3. Stand the test tube in the beaker of water. Put the thermometer into the test tube.
4. When the crystals have just melted remove the test tube from the water and start the clock.
5. Stand the test tube in the conical flask.
6. Stir the liquid in the tube all the time and take the temperature every half minute until the temperature has dropped to 38 °C.
7. Record your results in a table like this:

Time/ min	Temp/ °C
0	
½	
1	
1½	
2	

8. Record the temperature at which you first saw crystals forming.
9. Plot your results on a graph. The diagram shows you how to draw your axes.

WARNING

Be careful you do not push the thermometer through the glass of the test tube. Stir carefully.

WARNING

Before removing the thermometer from the test tube, put the test tube back in the beaker of water until the salol melts. Otherwise you may break the thermometer trying to remove it.

Finding out: Crystals from a solution

Potassium nitrate dissolves more in hot water than in cold. When a hot solution of potassium nitrate is cooled, crystals of potassium nitrate are formed. The size of the crystals formed depends on how quickly the solution is cooled.

Warning
Wear eye protection.

Instructions

1. Weigh out two 5 g samples of potassium nitrate.
2. Put one sample into each of two test tubes.
3. Half fill the beaker with water and heat the water to 40 °C.
4. Stand both test tubes in the beaker of water and shake them from time to time.
5. When all the potassium nitrate has dissolved, take one test tube, cork it and leave it to stand inside the conical flask until the next lesson.
6. Cool the other test tube by running it under the cold tap.
7. Compare the results of your experiments.

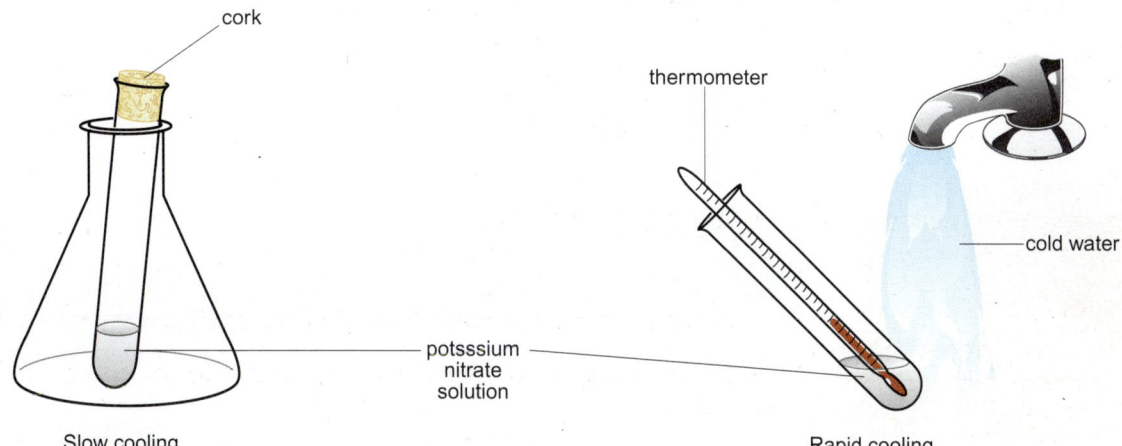

2.06 Colloids

When sugar is added to water the sugar **dissolves** to form a **solution**. You can see through a solution. A solution passes through a filter paper unchanged.

When powdered chalk is added to water the chalk does not dissolve. It forms a **suspension**. The chalk is spread throughout the water during mixing. The mixture is cloudy. When the mixture is left, the chalk settles.

Wallpaper paste is made of starch. When it is mixed with water it does not dissolve to form a solution. It stays spread out in the water and does not settle. It forms a jelly-like substance which is a special type of solution called a **colloid**.

A colloid is made of two substances which thoroughly mix but do not dissolve in each other. It is made up of tiny particles of one substance spread throughout the other.

Milk is an example of a colloid. It consists of tiny droplets of fat (or oil) spread or **dispersed** throughout the water. It is called an oil-in-water emulsion. The droplets of a colloid are between 0.01 mm and 0.000 001 mm wide. They are too large to dissolve but too small to settle.

Sometimes chemicals are added to a colloid to prevent different substances in the colloid from separating. These substances are called **emulsifying agents.** Look at the ingredients list on some of the foods you eat.

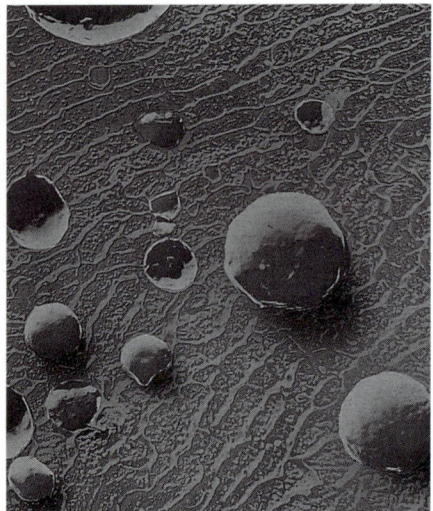

You can see the tiny droplets of fat in milk with a microscope

Can You?

50% of the volume of ice cream is air. When ice cream melts its volume decreases greatly. Plan and carry out an experiment to find out how much it decreases.

Different types of colloid

Type of colloid	Substance dispersed	Dispersion occurs in	Example
emulsion	liquid	liquid	milk, salad cream
sol	solid	liquid	wallpaper paste
foam	gas	liquid	whipped cream
gel	liquid	solid	fruit jelly

1. Here are some different mixtures.

   shaving cream   hair lotion   coffee   fly spray

   Copy and finish the table (right) using these mixtures as examples.

2. Butter is a water-in-oil emulsion. In what way is it different from milk?

3. The label on a bottle of salad cream gives the following ingredients: water, sugar, vinegar, sunflower oil, salt, lemon juice, mustard, lecithin, colouring.

   Lecithin is found in egg yolk. What job does it do in the salad cream?

Type of mixture	Contains	Example
solution	one substance dissolved in another	
foam	gas mixed with a liquid	
emulsion	two liquids which do not mix	
gel	liquid mixed with a solution	

Making a cake

2.07

Darren and Jo are going to make a sponge cake. Although they may not know it, they are carrying out a **chemical reaction**.

The pictures show what they must do.

a Stir 100 g of butter and 100 g of sugar together until the mixture is light and fluffy.

b Beat 2 eggs and add them to the mixture.

Did You Know?

Self-raising flour contains a raising agent which makes a cake rise during cooking. Plain flour does not contain a raising agent. The usual raising agent is bicarbonate of soda (its chemical name is sodium hydrogencarbonate).

e Remove from the oven and allow to cool.

d Put the mixture in a sponge tin and cook in the oven at 190 °C for 20 minutes.

c Add 100 g of self-raising flour and stir the mixture.

 All these questions refer to **Making a cake.**

1. Write out the list of ingredients they should use.
2. Why is it important to keep stirring throughout the stages **a**, **b** and **c**?
3. How will the mixture put into the tin in **d** be different from the cake taken out of the oven in **e**?
4. At which stage will a chemical reaction be taking place?
5. There are bubbles in the sponge cake. How are these bubbles formed?

31

2.08 Combustion

Having a bonfire

Some friends have built a bonfire for Guy Fawkes' night using materials that are being thrown away by people in the area. These materials can be called **fuel**.

When they built the bonfire, Barry said that the fuel should be dry. Jan said that the bonfire should be built so there are gaps at the bottom to let air in to help the fuel to burn.

When they came to light the bonfire, Ali used a firelighter and some paper to get it burning.

Combustion

Burning is a reaction of a fuel with oxygen in the air. Burning releases energy in the form of heat and light. **Combustion** is another word for burning.

The photograph on the left shows a large forest fire. For a fire to burn three things are needed – fuel, oxygen and heat. These are shown in the fire triangle below.

This forest fire is very difficult to put out.

> **Did You Know?**
>
> The most common household fire is due to a chip pan catching alight. The best way of putting it out is to put a wet cloth over the pan. Why does this put the fire out?

These are essential for a fire to burn.

1. Write down the two things the friends did to get their bonfire to burn well.

2. Here are some materials they were offered for the bonfire.

    cardboard   tree branches   bricks   newspaper
    scrap iron   plastic bags

    Which ones will burn and which will not burn?

3. Tony said that pouring petrol on the bonfire and setting light to it would be a better way to get it to burn. Why is Tony's idea **such** a bad one and one you should **never do**?

4. What ways are there to put out a forest fire? For each way, are you removing a fuel, oxygen or heat?

32

Mass changes on combustion

What is combustion?
Combustion is another name for burning. It is the reaction of a substance with oxygen from the air to form new substances and to release energy as heat and light.

Here are two examples of combustion.

Burning a piece of wood
The photographs below show a piece of wood before and after burning.

You will notice that when the piece of wood burns only a small amount of ash (and charcoal) is left.

During burning, gases are lost into the atmosphere

> **Did You Know?**
>
> Scientists two hundred years ago did accurate weighings on simple balances using a balancing beam. Despite very simple apparatus they were able to make accurate measurements.

You would probably think that the piece of wood weighs less after it has burned. Yes, the ash (and charcoal) does weigh less than the piece of wood. But if you managed to catch all of the gases that are lost and weighed everything, there would be an increase in mass.

Burning magnesium ribbon
Here is some information about burning a piece of magnesium ribbon in a crucible with a lid.

First of all the crucible and lid are weighed.

Then the crucible is heated.

Once they have cooled, the crucible and lid are weighed again.

Here is a set of results:

    mass of crucible and lid before heating   =   45.35 g

    mass of crucible and lid after heating   =   45.85 g

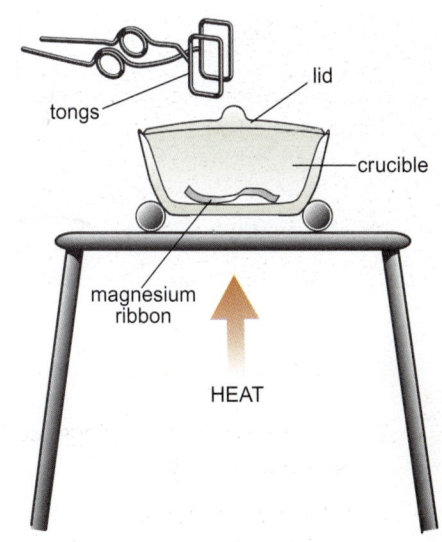

You can see that there has been a small increase in mass during burning. You can detect these small changes in mass during combustion reactions because weighing balance are very accurate.

---

1 Why do you think the lid is lifted off the crucible from time to time during the heating?

2 How does the mass change during the heating?

3 Why do you think there is a change of mass?

2.10 The discovery of oxygen

Joseph Priestley

Although oxygen is all around is it was not recognized until just over two hundred years ago. Oxygen was first discovered by a Swedish man called Wilhelm Scheele in 1773. He called oxygen 'fire air' because substances burn well in it. His book about his discovery did not come out until 1777.

In the meantime, in England, Joseph Priestley discovered oxygen without knowing anything about the work of Scheele. He reported his discovery at a public meeting of the British Royal Society in 1775. Because of this we usually give the credit for the discovery of oxygen to Priestley.

Priestley had been given an extremely large magnifying glass as a present. On 1 August 1774 he used the Sun and his magnifying glass to heat a number of substances.

One substance he heated was mercury. This is a silvery coloured liquid. Red powdery particles formed on the mercury. He carefully removed these particles and heated them alone. A colourless gas was produced.

He found that:

- a candle burned better in the gas than in air.
- a mouse in the gas was very lively.
- a piece of smouldering charcoal burst into flames in the gas.

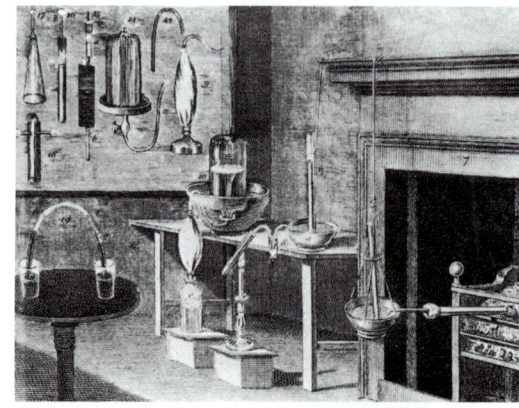
Priestley's laboratory

He called this gas, which we now call oxygen, 'dephlogisted air' – a rather lengthy name!

Priestley visited the famous French chemist Antoine Lavoisier in Paris and told him of his discovery. Lavoisier named the gas 'oxygen' in 1787. Priestley's discovery helped Lavoisier to develop his theory of combustion.

Did You Know?

Lavoisier was arrested in May 1794 during the French Revolution. After a brief trial he was guillotined and buried in a common grave. Priestley went to America where he had three sons and died peacefully.

---

1. What is the chemical name of the red powder Priestley heated?
2. Priestley was a teacher and a church minister. Although his scientific writings were well received, some of his religious writings were not. In addition to discovering oxygen he also studied the gas found over fermentation vats in a local brewery and a gas which he called 'phlogisticated air' which is the major component in air. Both of these gases put out a burning flame. What are these two gases?
3. Priestley wrote of oxygen: 'It may be peculiarly salutary for the lungs in certain cases.' Give one use of oxygen which Priestley could foresee.

The theory of combustion

2.11

In the eighteenth century it was believed that when something burns it loses a substance called 'phlogiston'. The residue remaining was called a 'calx'. This was called the **phlogiston theory**.

The famous French chemist Lavoisier did not believe this and wanted to establish a new theory to explain combustion. According to the phlogiston theory a substance that would not burn, e.g. sand, contained no phlogiston. This theory, however, did not explain why a substance such as mercury increases in mass when it loses phlogiston.

Lavoisier was very interested in Priestley's experiments and repeated them carefully. He heated some mercury for a number of days in the apparatus shown below.

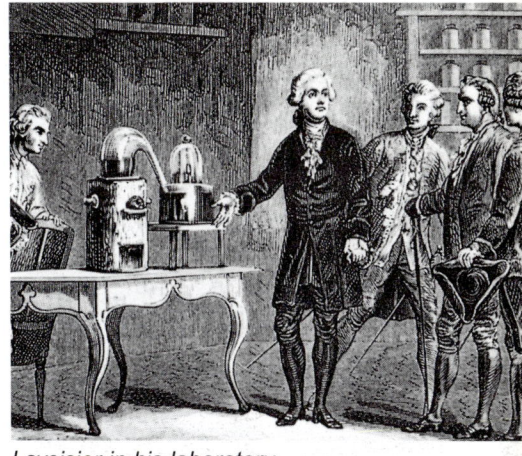

Lavoisier in his laboratory

> **Did You Know?**
>
> The word combust comes from the Latin word for burnt – *combustus*.

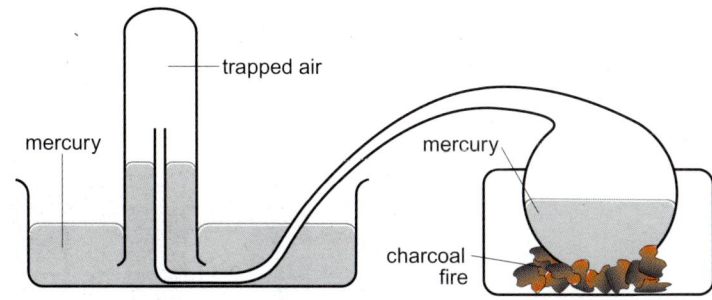

He noticed that approximately one-fifth of the air trapped had disappeared and a red powder was on the top of the mercury.

He carefully removed the red powder and weighed it. He then heated it alone and collected the gas which was produced. He also weighed the amount of mercury which had been produced.

He found that the red powder had decreased in mass. Also the volume of oxygen collected was the same as the volume of air which was lost in the first experiment.

Lavoisier concluded that the mercury increased in mass because it had combined with the oxygen in the air. Today we would summarize this as:

mercury + oxygen → mercury oxide

We now know that **combustion** is the reaction of a substance with oxygen. There is a release of energy in the form of heat and light.

---

1. What does this photograph of Lavoisier in his laboratory tell us about Lavoisier?

2. According to the phlogiston theory, which of the following substances:

   brick   wood   wood ash   petrol   pottery

   a contain no phlogiston
   b contain phlogiston
   c have lost their phlogiston?

3. Lavoisier heated mercury oxide and produced oxygen. Write a word equation for this reaction.

35

2.12 Acids, alkalis, indicators

Vinegar and lemon juice both have a sour taste. Substances with a sour taste contain an **acid.** Some substances containing acids cannot be tasted.

There is a test you can use to show whether a substance contains an acid. You can test for an acid or an alkali using an **indicator.** An indicator is a coloured solution usually made from a plant. You can make indicators from flowers (e.g. roses), fruit (blackberry) or parts of the plant (red cabbage).

One common indicator used is called **litmus.** It is made from a type of moss found in cold countries. It is made into a solution (called litmus solution) or soaked up and dried on paper (litmus paper).

The diagram shows a piece of red litmus paper and a piece of blue litmus paper being put into white vinegar. The blue litmus turns red in the vinegar. (The red litmus stays red.)

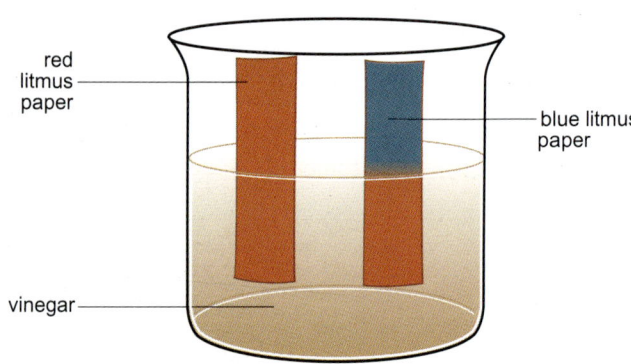
Litmus paper in white vinegar

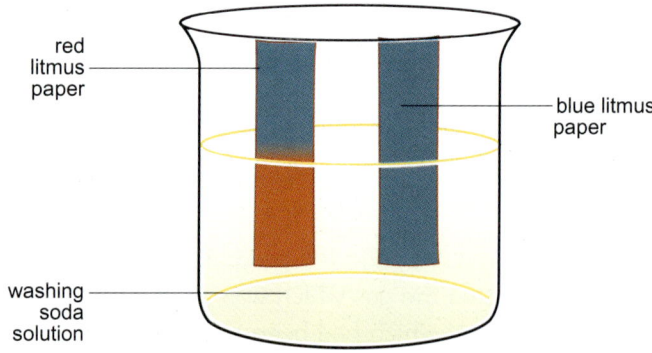
Litmus paper in washing soda solution

Substances opposite to acids are called **alkalis.** Washing soda is an example of an alkali. You can see from the diagram that when red and blue litmus paper are added to a solution of washing soda, the red litmus turns blue and the blue litmus stays blue.

When red and blue litmus paper are added to pure water, the red litmus paper stays red and the blue litmus paper stays blue. Water is not an acid or an alkali. It is said to be **neutral.**

Flowers as Indicators

Many coloured flowers contain chemicals that act as indicators. However, yellow flowers like daffodils and crocuses do not work. Pink and red roses work well but yellow roses do not.

1. What happens to the litmus paper in vinegar?
2. What happens to litmus paper in washing soda solution?
3. Pure water is exactly neutral. Rainwater is slightly acidic. Tap water is often slightly alkaline. Suggest why rainwater and tap water are not always neutral.

Finding out: Red cabbage as an indicator

An indicator is a coloured substance which can be used to detect acidic or alkaline solutions by changing colour. In this experiment dye from red cabbage is being extracted and used as an indicator.

Instructions

1. Heat about 300 cm^3 of water in the larger beaker until the water is boiling. Turn off the gas supply to extinguish the Bunsen burner.

2. Put about 5 cm depth of shredded red cabbage into the boiling tube and just cover with ethanol. Warm the mixture by dipping the boiling tube into the beaker of hot water. Extra ethanol can be added.

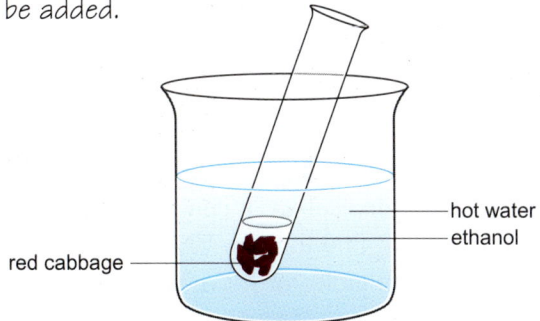

3. Filter the solution into the small beaker to remove the remains of red cabbage.

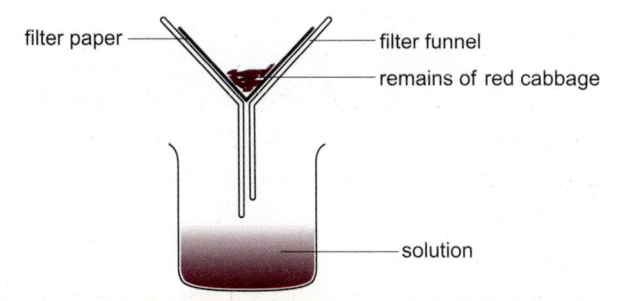

WARNING

Acids and alkalis are very corrosive. Goggles should be worn throughout this experiment.

Ethanol is very flammable. Never heat it with a Bunsen burner. Here it is heated in a test tube in beaker of hot water with all flames extinguished.

4. Divide this solution into four portions in four separate test tubes.

5. Add something to each test tube as follows:

   Test Tube 1 Add an equal volume of dilute sulphuric acid (an acid).

   Test Tube 2 Add an equal volume of dilute sodium hydroxide solution (an alkali).

   Test Tube 3 Add an equal volume of solution X.

   Test Tube 4 Add an equal volume of solution Y.

   Note the colours of the solutions in the four test tubes.

6. Copy the following table and write down your results in it.

Test tube	Solution added	Colour of Solution
1	Sulphuric acid	
2	Sodium hydroxide	
3	X	
4	Y	

7.
   a. What colour does the red cabbage extract solution turn in an acid?
   b. What colour does the red cabbage extract solution turn in an alkali?
   c. Is solution X an acid or an alkali?
   d. Is solution Y an acid or an alkali?

2.13 Acid and alkali strength

Acids and alkalis vary greatly in strength. Vinegar is a weak acid and sulphuric acid is a strong acid. Litmus tells us whether a substance is an acid, an alkali or a neutral substance. It does not tell us how strong an acid or alkali is.

pH scale

The strength of an acid or an alkali is measured on the **pH scale.** This is a scale from 1 to 14.

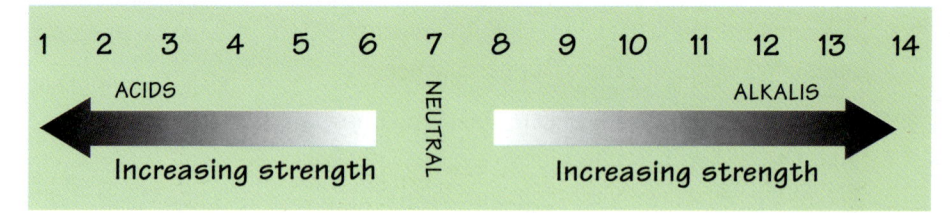

The pH scale shows how strong an acid or alkali is

The pH value of a solution can be found using a pH meter. The probe of the meter is put into the solution and the pH value is shown on a digital readout or a scale.

Another way of finding the pH of a solution is to use **universal indicator.** This is a mixture of several indicators. It changes through a range of colours and from the colour you can find the pH. The illustration below shows the colours of a simple universal indicator for measuring pH.

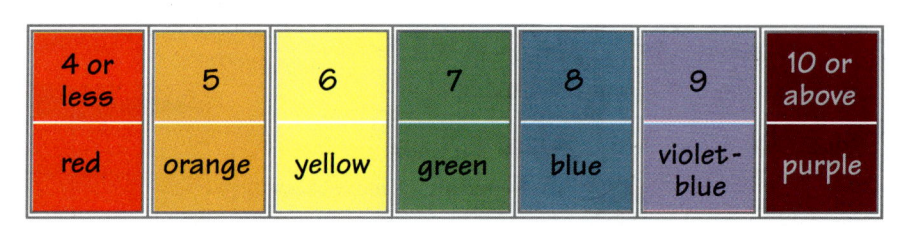

4 or less	5	6	7	8	9	10 or above
red	orange	yellow	green	blue	violet-blue	purple

Using a pH meter

Colour chart for universal indicator

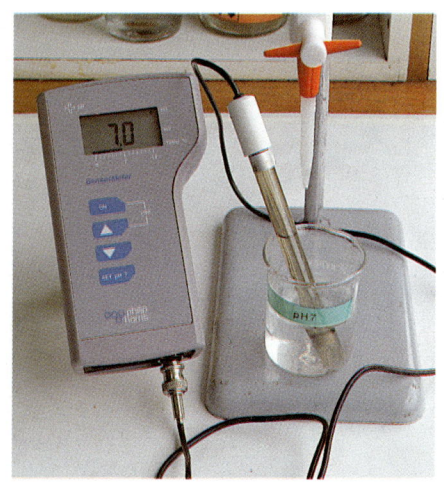

---

1 Choose words from the list to complete the sentences.

neutral   strong acid   strong alkali
weak acid   weak alkali

a A solution with a pH value of 7 is _____.

b A solution with a pH value of 12 is a _____.

c A solution with a pH value of 6 is a _____.

2 What colour does universal indicator go in a solution with a pH value of

a 4   b 7   c 8   d 11?

3 Why is it very difficult to measure the pH value of blackcurrant juice with universal indicator?

4 Why is it difficult to measure the pH value of household bleach using universal indicator?

Carbonates and acid

2.14

Many rocks contain chemicals called carbonates. You can tell if a rock contains a carbonate by adding a few drops of acid. If a carbonate is present, the rock will fizz when the acid is added and bubbles of a gas will be seen to escape. This gas is carbon dioxide.

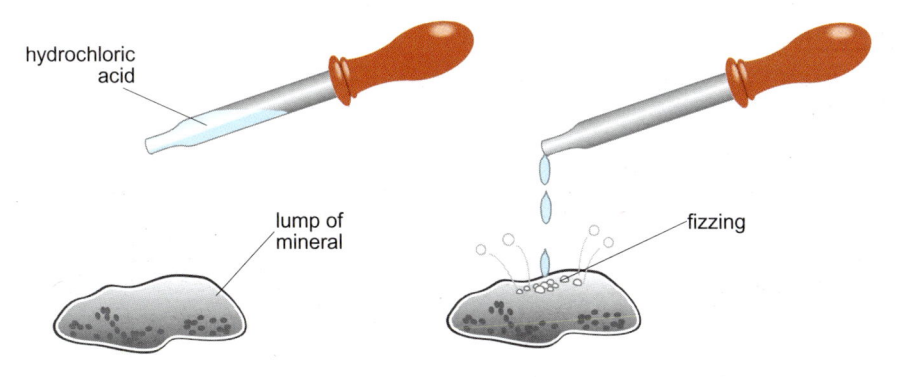

> **Did You Know?**
>
> Carbonate rocks are usually the remains of animals with shells trapped in the Earth millions of years ago.

The diagram below shows how you can test this gas. The gas produced can be passed through a delivery tube into a solution of limewater. Limewater is colourless at the start, but quickly turns white and cloudy when carbon dioxide bubbles through it. This is used as the test for carbon dioxide.

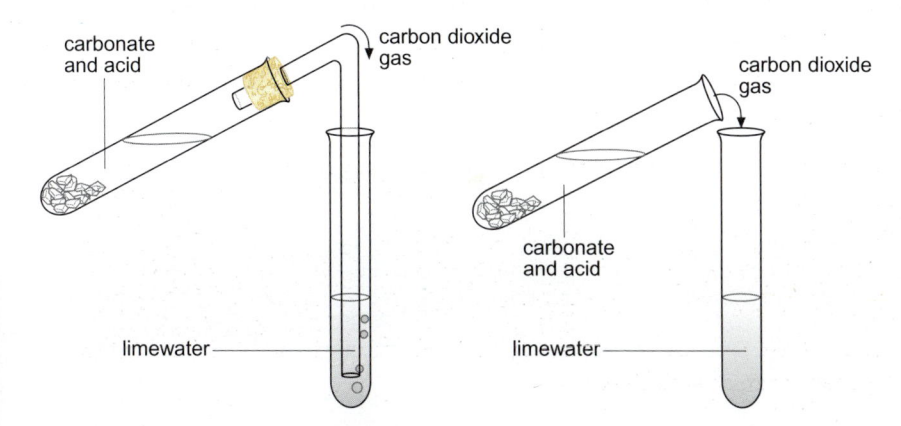

Testing for carbon dioxide with limewater

Carbon dioxide can be poured from one test tube to another. This is possible because carbon dioxide is heavier than air. You cannot see this because carbon dioxide is a colourless gas.

1 A student has a test tube which he thinks contains carbon dioxide gas. He puts a burning splint into the gas. The splint goes out.

   a Why does this not prove the gas is carbon dioxide?

   b What should he do to prove it is carbon dioxide?

2 Fire extinguishers often contain carbon dioxide. Suggest two reasons why.

39

Finding out: Heating substances

Substances may change on heating. When a change does take place, the substance may stay as it is when the hot tube is cooled or there may be a further change.

Instructions

1 Put one spatula measure of ammonium chloride into a test tube.

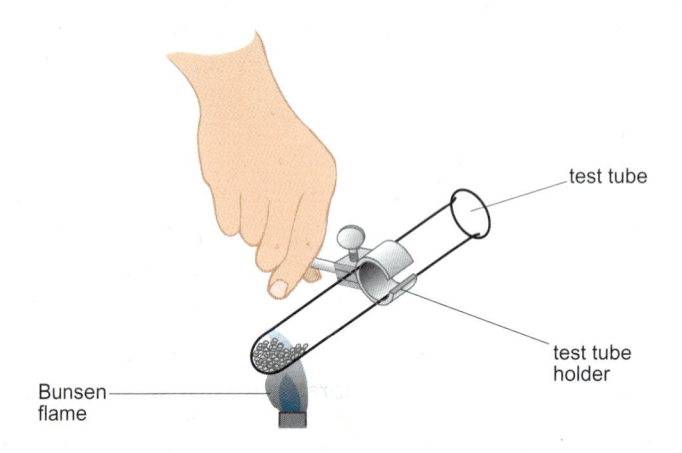

2 Heat this test tube gently at first, noting down any changes that occur.

3 Allow the test tube to cool, noting any changes that occur.

4 Repeat with the other four substances.

5 Put your results into a table like the one below.

Substance	Appearance before heating	Change on heating	Change on cooling
ammonium chloride			
copper carbonate			
zinc oxide			
sand			
polythene (small amount)			

6 Which of these five substances is unchanged on heating?

7 Explain what happens when ammonium chloride is heated.

8 Which one of the substances heated changes permanently?

Physical and chemical changes 2.15

The previous fourteen sections of this book have been about changes. As you look back you will find many examples of changes from one material to another. We can divide changes into two types.

Physical or temporary changes.
These are changes which take place which can be easily reversed. The word temporary means 'not lasting'. For example, if you put some water into a freezer, the liquid water will change to ice. If, however, you take the ice out of the freezer it will melt and water will re-form.

Chemical or permanent changes.
These are changes which cannot be reversed. Once they have taken place the original material cannot be re-formed. The word permanent means 'for ever'. If you burn a piece of wood, a flame is seen and some energy is lost as heat and light. The resulting ash cannot be turned back into wood.

The pictures below show two changes taking place. Try to decide whether these changes are physical (temporary) or chemical (permanent).

Did You Know?

Permanent changes can take place very quickly or very slowly. An explosion takes place in a tiny fraction of a second, but some processes of rock formation take millions of years.

When a firework burns, a chemical reaction takes place and a chemical (or permanent change) takes place. When water in a kettle boils, the water turns to steam. However, on a cool surface in the same room, for example a window, the water will re-form. The steam condenses and re-forms water. Boiling water is a physical (or temporary) change.

1. What name is given to a change which is easily reversed?
2. What name is given to a change which is not easily reversed?
3. Here are some of the changes which you may have already met.

   Which of these changes are chemical (permanent) and which are physical (temporary)?

   a Dissolving some sugar in water.
   b Burning a piece of magnesium.
   c Heating mercury oxide.
   d Forming crystals by allowing a liquid to cool and solidify.
   e Making a sponge cake.
4. Find some other examples of physical and chemical change.

41

CHAPTER 3

3.01

ELECTRICITY/ CHARGE

Electricity on the move

Bringing electricity home

Why do we need pylons? They hold up the wires that bring **electricity** to our homes. They are made from strong **metals** such as steel.

Metals allow electricity to pass through them easily. That is why they are called **conductors.** If the wires touch the pylon, electricity passes down to the ground and is wasted.

In the photograph you can see how the wires hang from the pylon. They are held in place by materials that do not allow electricity to pass through them. These materials are called **insulators.**

Conductors and insulators are both needed to bring electricity to our homes safely.

Using electricity at home

Your walkman uses batteries. Batteries are safe, they do not give you a shock when you touch them. **Mains electricity** is dangerous, it can kill if used wrongly.

Wires, sockets and plugs are used to connect things to the mains safely. Wires need to have metal parts that allow the electricity to pass easily. They also need to be covered with an insulator so that you do not get a shock if you touch them. The wires and the insulator need to be bendy.

Plugs and sockets do not need to be bendy. They use hard plastic or rubber to protect you from the metal parts that carry the electricity.

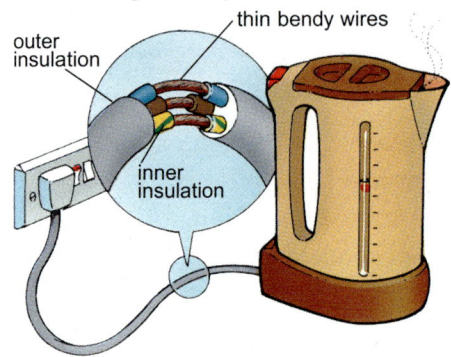

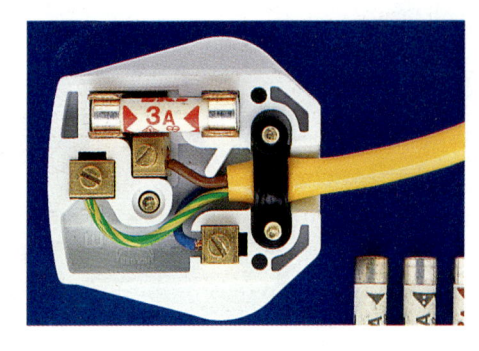

Did You Know?

The wires that the pylons support are mainly aluminium because it is light. They are separated from the pylons by insulators made from porcelain or glass.

---

outer insulation
thin bendy wires
inner insulation

---

1 Make a copy of this table.

Conductors	Insulators

Write each material from the list in the correct column.

brass   copper   cork   glass
gold   iron   plastic   wood
silver polythene

2 How can you test a material to find out if it is a conductor?

  a Draw what you would do.

  b What happens if the material is a conductor?

42

Circuits and symbols

The need for electrical diagrams

Here is a drawing of a circuit that you might have made. It shows two **cells**, two **lamps** and a **switch**. You probably call a cell a **battery**, but the word battery is really a name for two or more cells used together.

As you study science you need to keep a record of what you do and what you see. That way you can look back and check to see if your ideas fit in with what happens.

Keeping a record of all the circuits you make could be a long process, so you need to learn an easy way to draw the circuits you make. Once you have learnt the electrical symbols you can draw a **circuit diagram** very quickly. You will then have more time to do experiments.

Some symbols

The **symbols** on the right are for the **components** you have already used to build circuits. You will learn more symbols as you need them.

Using these symbols, the circuit drawn above looks like this (below right).

Notice how connecting wires are drawn as straight lines. The circles and lines in this diagram were drawn using a computer, but you can draw your circuit diagrams freehand.

When connecting together circuits in science, you should always work from a circuit diagram in your notebook. That way, you can tick off components such as lamps and connecting wires as you connect them into your circuit.

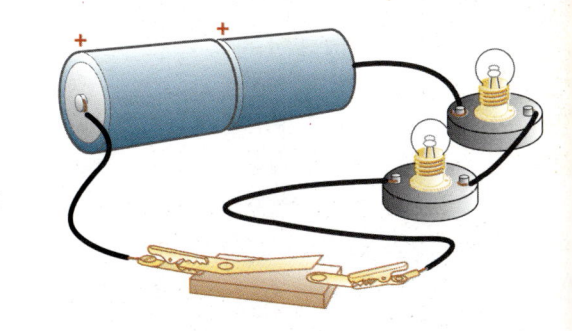

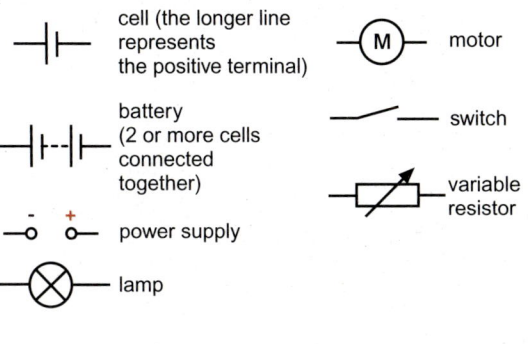

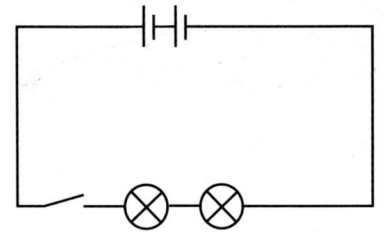

---

1 Draw this as a circuit diagram using the symbols shown above.

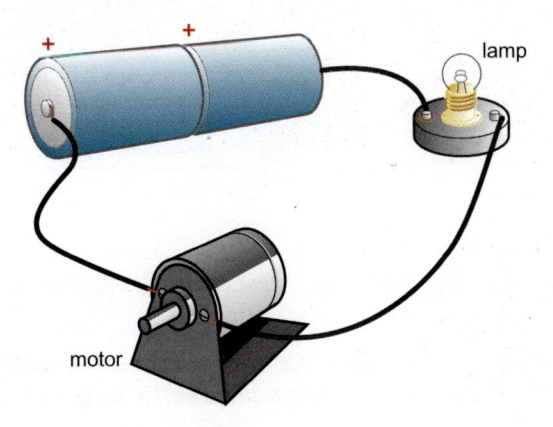

2 A torch is made from two cells, a switch and a lamp. Draw a circuit diagram showing how they could be connected together.

3 In the circuit below, when the switch is pressed the lamp does not light.

  a What is wrong with the circuit?

  b Redraw the circuit diagram, so that the lamp lights when the switch is pressed.

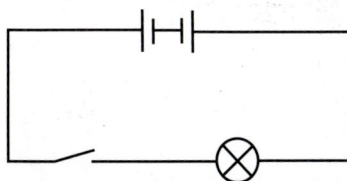

4 Draw two circuit diagrams using a lamp, a battery and two switches.

  a The lamp should only light when **both** switches are pressed.

  b The lamp should light when either one switch or the other is pressed.

43

3.03 Using switches

Different types of switch

Switches are used to turn things on and off. The photos on the left show several different types of switch.

- A **light switch** has two positions. Whichever position it is put in, it stays there. When in the 'on' position, the switch terminals are joined by a thick copper strip. In the 'off' position they are separated by an air gap.

- A **bell push** is normally in the 'off' position. It only stays in the 'on' position when you press it with your finger. One contact is springy to return it to 'off' when you let go.

- **Reed switches** are very useful in burglar alarms. They are operated by magnets. When a magnet is held close to the switch the contacts close, as shown in the diagram left. The contacts open when the magnet is taken away. A reed switch can be fitted into a door frame or a window frame with a magnet fitted into the door or opening part of the window. If the door or window is opened, the reed switch contacts open and the alarm is set off.

Switches in circuits

There is only one current path in a series circuit. If there is a break anywhere in the path the circuit is switched off. In the series circuit shown left the lamp and the motor have to be both on or both off. A switch can be placed anywhere in the circuit to switch them on and off.

Parallel circuits can have switches that control individual devices. They can also have a master switch that can turn everything off.

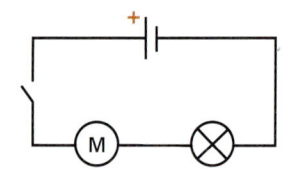

1. The switches in the diagram on the right have been labelled S1, S2 and S3.
   a. Which switch controls the motor only?
   b. Which switch controls the lamp only?
   c. What is the purpose of the third switch?

2. What acts as the insulator between the contacts when a bell-push is switched off?

3. Design a burglar alarm circuit that uses two reed switches, one fixed in each of two doors. The alarm should sound when either door is opened.

4. The inside light in a car is switched on by opening either the driver's door or the passenger door. It uses switches that turn 'on' when a door is opened. Draw a circuit diagram to show how the circuit works.

Did You Know?

In some switches the contacts are plated with gold or silver. These do not corrode as readily as copper or brass so they are more reliable and last longer.

Measuring current — 3.04

What is current?

Electricity is a very useful **energy source.** We use it for heating and lighting the places we live and work in. It also makes motors turn round, so we use it to produce movement in washing machines and vacuum cleaners.

When we use electricity for heating, lighting or movement **electric current** passes in the wires. This makes things like kettles, lamps and motors do their jobs.

Kettles need a lot of electric current, so they have thick wires connecting them to the electricity mains. If you look at a bedside lamp or a table lamp, you will see that the connecting wires are thin. This is because only a small current is needed for things that produce light.

These everyday objects produce heat, light and movement when electric current passes in them.

Measuring current

Electric current is measured using an **ammeter**. This measures how much current is passing in a wire. Current is measured in **amperes** or **amps** (A) for short. The current passing in a kettle element is about 10 amps (10 A).

The pictures on the right show two different types of ammeter. One displays the numbers on a small screen. The other has a pointer that moves over a scale.

The diagram below shows how to connect an ammeter to measure the current that passes into a lamp. You could also use the ammeter to measure how much current passes out of the lamp.

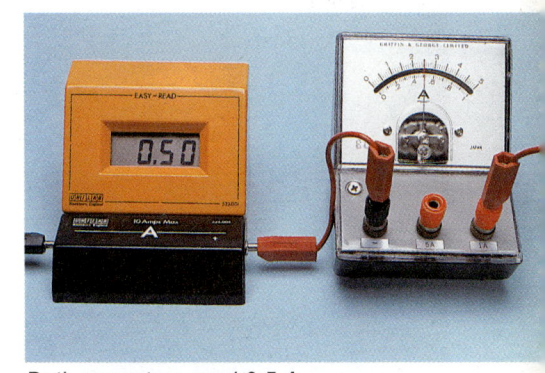

Both ammeters read 0.5 A

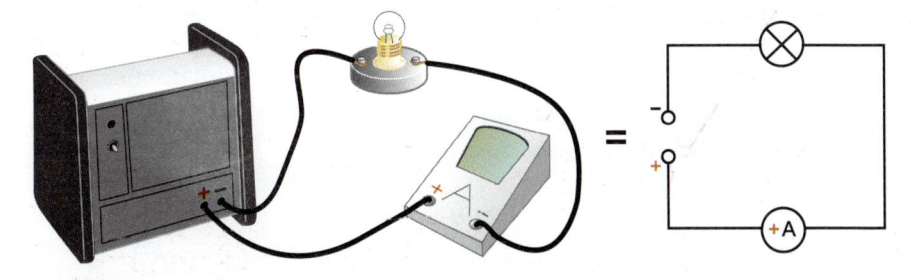

---

1. Write down the names of three things that produce heat when an electric current passes in them.
2. Why do kettles need thick wires to connect them to the mains supply but lamps only need thin wires?
3. The table shows the current that passes in some things when switched on and working normally.

    a Which appliance has the greatest current passing in it?

    b Which appliance needs the thinnest connecting wires?

    c Draw a bar chart to illustrate the information in the table.

Appliance	Current
microwave oven	5 A
hairdryer	6 A
toaster	4 A
television	1.5 A

3.05 A series of things

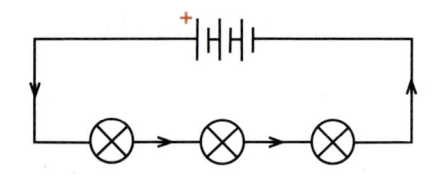

One thing after another

Lamps and cells can be wired in **series**. The diagram on the left shows three cells and three lamps all connected in series.

There is only one possible path for the current in a series circuit. This is shown by the arrows on the circuit diagram. Electric current is always drawn as passing from the **positive** terminal to the **negative** one.

If you were to use this circuit as a lighting circuit for a younger brother or sister's toy house you would find that it has one major drawback. Unscrewing one lamp causes all three to go out. This is one reason why series circuits are not used for lighting at home; if they were you would have to have either all the lights on or none of the lights on.

Christmas tree lights

Some Christmas tree lights use a series circuit to use twenty or more low voltage lamps from the mains supply. When a lamp 'blows', the filament, the part that gets hot and gives out light, breaks. If all the Christmas tree lights suddenly go out, there is no easy way to tell which lamp filament has broken. To avoid this happening, the manufacturers of the lamps try to make them so that current can still pass when the filament breaks. This means that only the 'blown' lamp goes out, so you can easily tell which one to replace.

These Christmas lights are in series

Using a battery

The type of cell that you use in a walkman or a torch has a **voltage** of 1.5 **volts**. When a higher voltage is needed two or more cells are connected in series to make a battery. Two of these cells in series make a 3 V (2 x 1.5) battery and six make a 9 V (6 x 1.5) battery.

1. Which circuit shows a lamp and a motor connected in series?

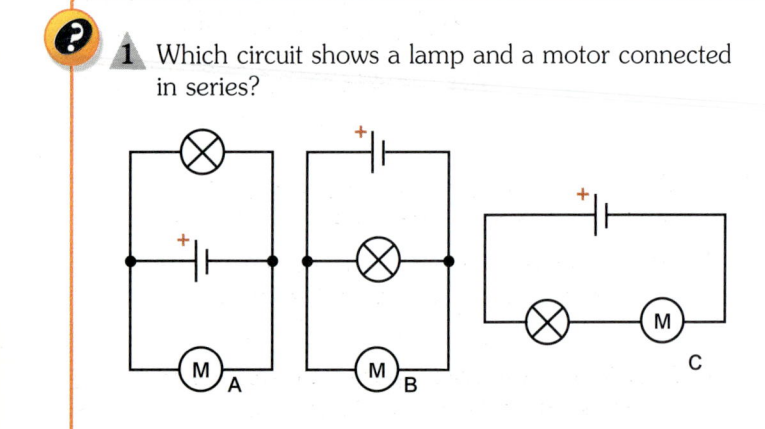

2. a How many 1.5 V cells are needed to make a 12 V battery?
   b Draw a diagram to show how they should be connected.

3. A torch has two cells, a lamp and a switch all connected in series.
   a Draw a circuit diagram of the torch.
   b Draw arrows on your circuit diagram to show the current path.

Current in series circuits

3.06

The current in a lamp
When an ammeter is used to measure the current passing in a device such as a lamp, the ammeter and lamp are wired in series. The current has to pass in both the ammeter and the lamp, connected one after the other.

Ammeter readings taken of the current in the wires each side of the lamp show that the current leaving the lamp is the same as the current that enters. In other words, lamps and other devices do not use up electric current.

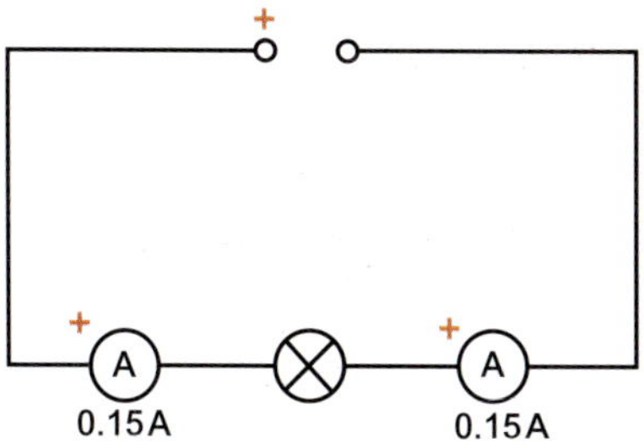

Putting lamps in series
When more lamps are added to the circuit shown right, you will notice two things: each lamp is dimmer than the single lamp on its own; the ammeter reading goes down. Both things show that less current is passing in the circuit.

The job of the current is to transfer **energy** from the cells to the lamps. Less current means that less energy is transferred each second. And more lamps in the circuit mean that each lamp gets a smaller share of this energy. These are two reasons why adding more lamps in a series circuit makes them dimmer.

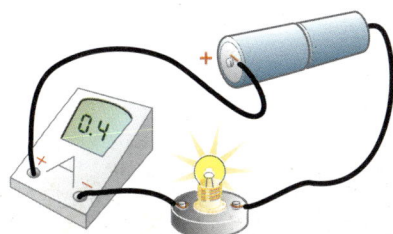

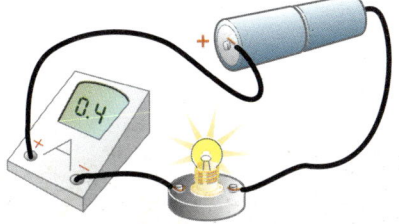

This lamp is bright ...

Using a series resistor
Light emitting diodes (LEDS) are used to indicate whether a circuit is switched on. They are also used in some digital clocks. Often the voltage supply in a circuit is too high for an LED; it would cause too much current for the LED, which would 'blow'.

To get round this another component, called a **resistor**, is used in the circuit. It is wired in series with the LED. The job of the resistor is to limit the current that passes in the circuit.

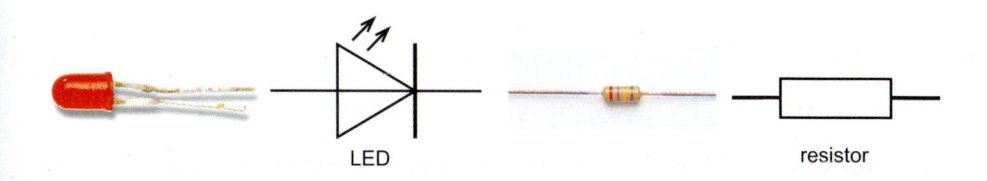

but these are dim...

LED

resistor

Did You Know?
The wire filament in an ordinary lamp is more than one metre long. The electric current heats the filament to a temperature of 2500 °C.

---

1 Write down the reading on ammeters A1 and A2.

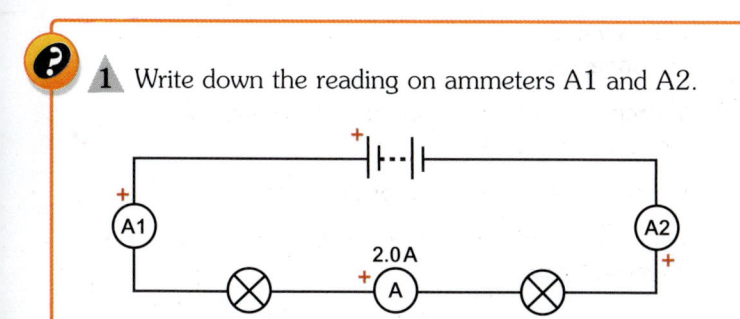

2 a Draw a circuit diagram showing a lamp and a motor connected in series with a battery.

b What difference is there in the speed of the motor if it is connected on its own to the battery?

c Explain why the motor speed is different when it is connected on its own to the battery.

Finding out: Current in series circuits

The diagram and the circuit diagram each show two lamps in series with a power supply and an ammeter. The ammeter is measuring the current that passes from the positive terminal of the power supply.

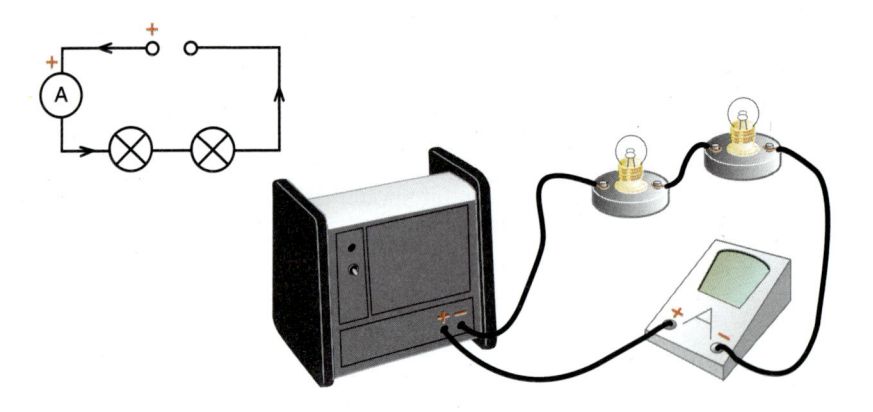

Instructions

1. Make up the circuit and write down the ammeter reading in your notebook. Use a table like this:

Ammeter position	Ammeter reading in A
between + terminal and first lamp	
between the two lamps	
between the second lamp and − terminal	

2. Place the ammeter in the other two positions shown in the table and write down the readings in the table.

3. Answer these questions in your notebook.

   a. What have you found out about how the current changes in the circuit?

   b. Do the lamps use up electric current? Explain how you can tell.

In parallel

3.07

One or the other

A series circuit has only one path for the current to take. When there is more than one current path round a circuit it is called a **parallel** circuit. There are three possible paths for the current to take in this circuit. Can you identify them?

Remember that current passes from positive to negative in a circuit. In the circuit shown on the right the current passes in an anticlockwise direction. Some current passes in the top lamp, some passes in the motor and some passes in the bottom lamp. Each of the three devices works independently, unlike those in a series circuit. If any one of them breaks or is disconnected it does not affect the others. Provided that the battery or power supply is capable of supplying enough current, any number of devices can be connected in parallel and be working at the same time.

A parallel circuit

Using parallel circuits

Some Christmas tree lights use a series circuit. Others use a parallel circuit, with a number of lamps all being connected in parallel to a low voltage transformer. These have the advantage that all the lamps work independently, so if one lamp filament breaks the others carry on working normally. A broken lamp is easily spotted and replaced. They are more expensive to buy than the series type, because of the additional cost of the transformer.

Parallel circuits are used in cars to connect all the lights, windscreen wipers and other electrical devices to the low voltage supply. A major advantage of using parallel circuits is that they allow each device to have its own switch and to be switched on and off without affecting other things that are connected to the same voltage supply.

The lighting circuit in a house is a parallel circuit. The circuit diagram on the right shows how four lamps can be connected to the same mains supply but be switched on and off independently. Each lamp could be in a different room in a house and have its own switch, so that the lighting in any one room is not affected by that in the other rooms.

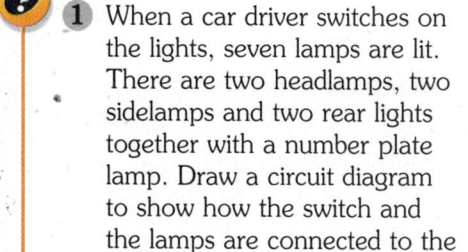

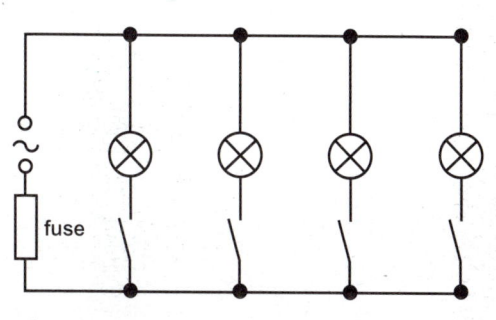

A mains lighting circuit where each lamp has its own switch

1. When a car driver switches on the lights, seven lamps are lit. There are two headlamps, two sidelamps and two rear lights together with a number plate lamp. Draw a circuit diagram to show how the switch and the lamps are connected to the car battery.

2. A toy house has two upstairs rooms and two downstairs rooms. Design a battery-operated lighting system for the house and draw a wiring plan.

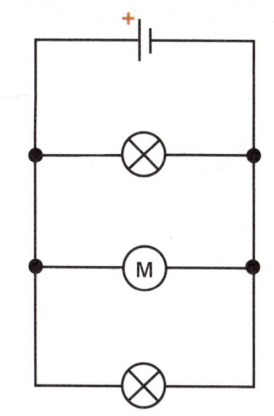

Danger?

It is dangerous to tamper with mains electricity. Thirty people are killed in Britain each year trying to do their own electrical repairs and maintenance. It should always be left to the experts.

49

3.08 Current in parallel circuits

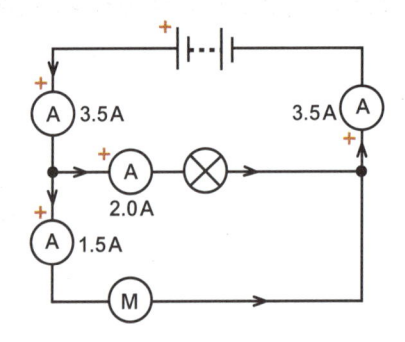

There is only one path for the current in a series circuit, so the current has to be the same everywhere. A parallel circuit has more than one current path, with current splitting and rejoining at junctions. The ammeter readings in the diagram on the left show what happens to the current at these junctions.

The current divides at the junction, some passing in the lamp and some passing in the motor. If you add together the currents that pass in the lamp and the motor, you find that the total current coming out of the junction is equal to the current that goes in.

You learned in 3.06 Current in series circuits that components such as lamps and motors do not use up current, so it should be no surprise that the same rule applies to junctions in a parallel circuit.

Putting lamps in parallel

The diagram below shows what happens to the total current when more lamps are added in parallel to a circuit.

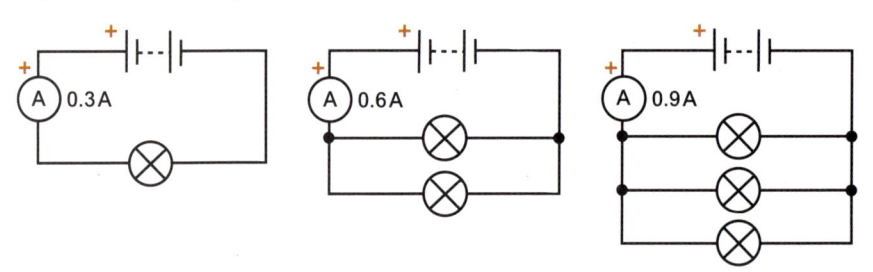

Adding an additional lamp to a parallel circuit does not affect the lamps already there. The current from the battery or power supply increases when an extra lamp is added in parallel. The amount of increase is the new current that passes in the extra lamp.

Did You Know?

Before ammeters were invented, scientists measured electric currents by the size of the twitch produced when the current was passed through a frog's leg.

---

1. Write down the current passing in each of the ammeters A1 to A3 in the diagram below.

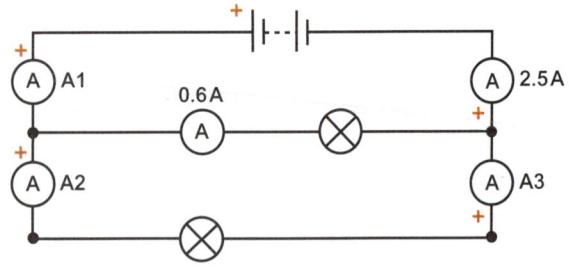

2. An electric fire has three heating elements wired in parallel. When switched on, the current in each element is 4A.

   a What are the advantages of wiring the elements in parallel?

   b Calculate the size of the current that passes in the mains cable when all three elements are switched on.

   c The fire has two switches. One switch operates two elements and the other operates a third. Draw a circuit diagram showing how the heating elements are connected to the mains supply.

3. A hairdryer has two heating elements and a fan.

   a Why should the fan *always* be on when a heating element is on?

   b Suggest how the fan motor and the heating elements should be connected so that the heating elements cannot be on without the fan.

Finding out: Current in parallel circuits

The diagrams show a parallel circuit with two current paths. They show how to connect an ammeter to measure the current in one lamp only.

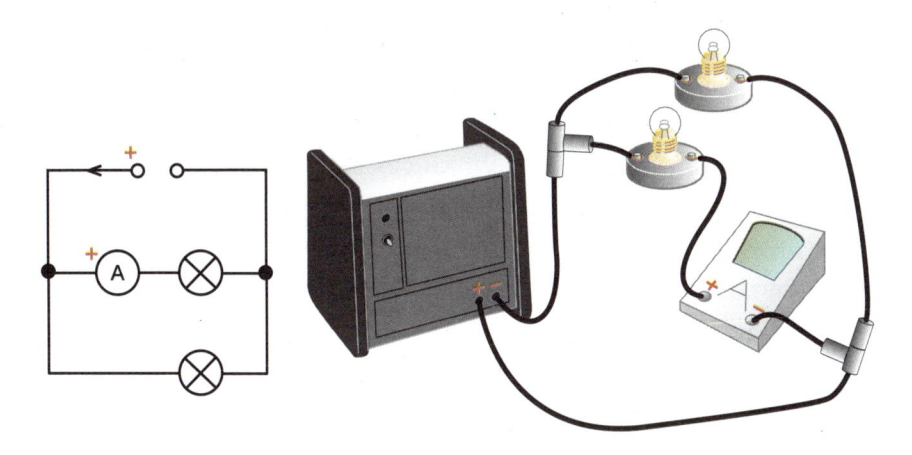

Instructions

1 Make up the circuit and write down the ammeter reading.

2 Use a table like this:

Current being measured	Ammeter reading in A
current in first lamp only	
current in second lamp only	
current passing out of power supply	
current returning to power supply	

3 Place the ammeter to measure the other three currents in the table, one at a time.

4 Examine your results and write down a rule about the amount of current that passes into a junction and the amount that passes out.

3.09 How bright?

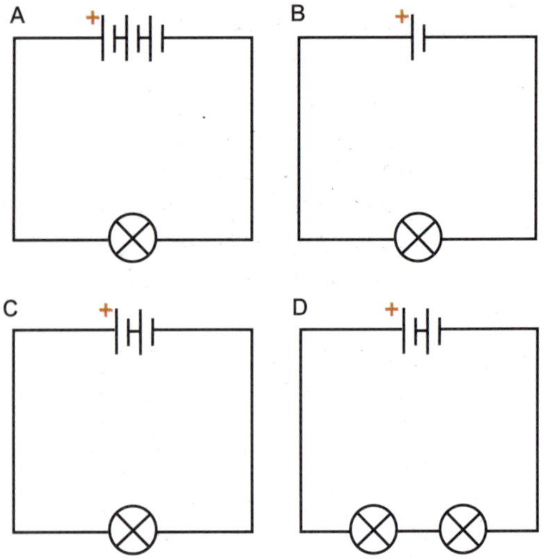

What makes a lamp bright or dim?

When you use a torch the lamp gets dimmer as the batteries run down. Replacing the battery or cells with new ones makes it bright again. What else, apart from the condition of the cells, makes a lamp bright or dim?

One thing is the **voltage**, the size of the push from the cells. Another thing that can affect the brightness is how many lamps there are. Two lamps together in a circuit (D left) like this are **in series**. The electricity has to pass through one after the other. The more lamps that are added in series, the dimmer they become. Which circuit on the left will give the brightest lamp?

It is harder for electricity to pass through the long, thin filament wires in a lamp than it is to pass through the short, fat connecting wires. The wires in the filament **resist** the electricity more than the connecting wires do. If the electricity has to pass through two filaments one after the other, there is more **resistance** than when it has to pass through just one.

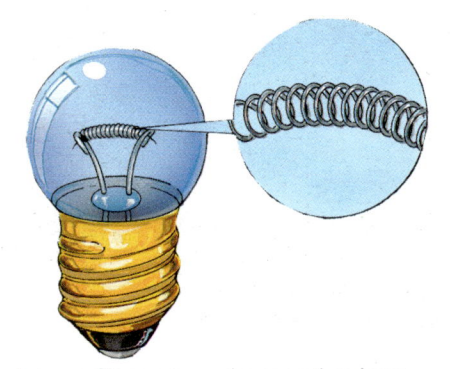

The lamp dimmer

The diagram below shows a circuit that uses a **variable resistor** to change the brightness of a lamp. When the slider is moved, the lamp becomes brighter or dimmer. If you have a lamp dimmer switch at home, this uses a variable resistor along with other components to change the brightness of the lamp. The variable resistor shown in the diagram works by changing the amount of resistance in the circuit.

Moving the slider in one direction increases the resistance, so less electricity passes, making the lamp dimmer. If you move the slider in the opposite direction the resistance becomes less, so more electricity passes round the circuit and the lamp is brighter.

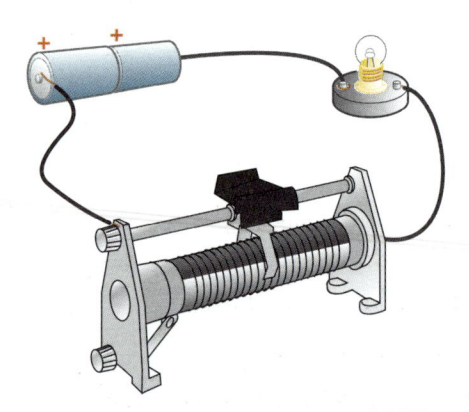

A lamp filament can be over 1 m long

Did You Know?

Variable resistors are used as volume controls on radios, televisions and hi-fis.

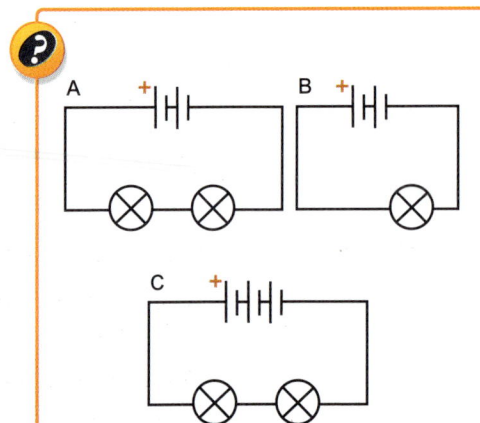

1. In the circuits on the left which lamp is brightest (A,B,C)? Explain why this one is brightest.

2. Design a circuit that uses a variable resistor to change the speed of a motor.

3. A variable resistor is made by winding one metre of wire into a coil. Explain how moving the slider along the coil changes the resistance in the circuit.

Getting charged up

3.10

Fun with balloons

If you rub a balloon on your sweater, you can make it stick to a wall or a ceiling. Rubbing the balloon gives it an **electric charge**. This makes it attracted to some things. Try holding a charged balloon near someone's hair or some scraps of paper. It pulls the hair or paper towards it, showing that there is an **attractive force**.

The charged balloon pulls the person's hair

The balloon pulls the pieces of paper

You should experiment to find out which materials are attracted to a charged balloon. If you have two balloons you can experiment with a different force. Rub one balloon on your sweater and put it on a table top. Then rub another balloon on your sweater. Now use it to push the first balloon. See how they push away from each other. This pushing away force is called **repulsion.** It is the opposite to the force of attraction.

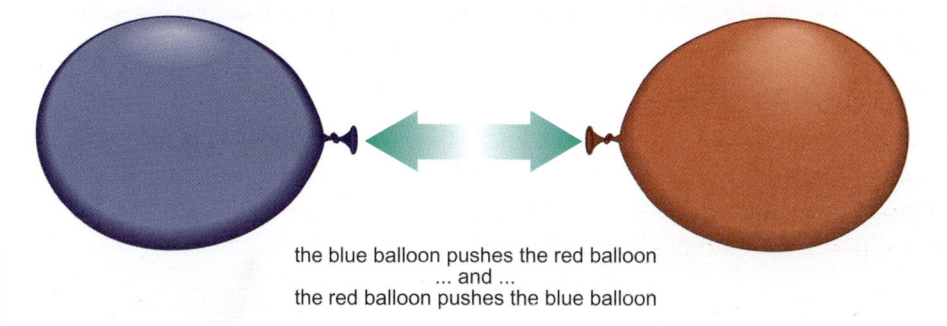

the blue balloon pushes the red balloon
... and ...
the red balloon pushes the blue balloon

The forces between two charged balloons

Did You Know?

Van de Graaff generators can create very high voltages, up to five million volts. Scientists use them to study lightning by causing huge sparks to pass through the air.

A van de Graaff generator can be used to show that like charges repel - the results are quite dramatic

---

1 Fit each word from the list into the correct blank space in the paragraph.

charged   hair   sweater

Rubbing a balloon with a _____ makes it become charged. A _____ balloon attracts small pieces of paper and the _____ on a person's head.

2 A duster is used to rub a balloon.

When a duster is held near to the charged balloon, they attract each other.

Draw a diagram showing the duster near the balloon.

Draw force arrows on the duster and the balloon.

Write a sentence to describe each force.

3 When a car is filled with petrol, electric charge can collect on the car body.

This can cause a spark if someone stands close to it.

Explain why this spark could be dangerous.

53

CHAPTER 4

4.01

VARIATION, CLASSIFICATION, AND KEYS

These twins look different even though they have identical genes

Telling individuals apart in this flock is not easy!

These snails show a wide range of designs due to different genes

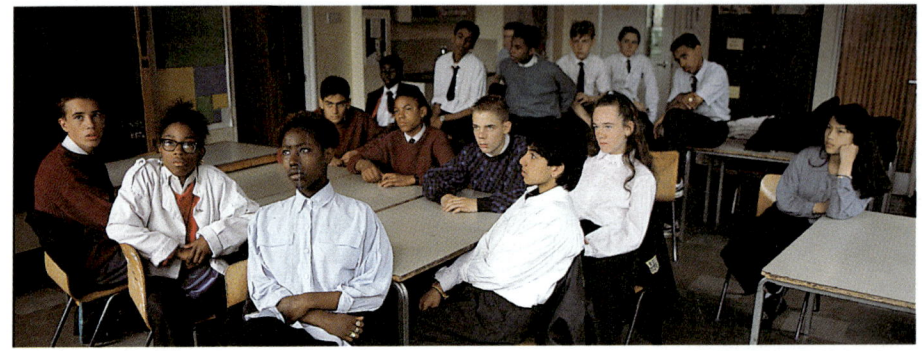

Everyone is different

Look at your neighbour. He or she is different from you. Each person in your school is easy to recognise. Now think about the cats you may see in your area. Are they all different? It is usually easy to tell them apart. What about a flock of starlings? For us, they are quite difficult to tell apart. Regular bird watchers can tell individuals apart. The slightly different size or shape; the differences in feather colour or markings are all tell-tale signs.

In living things each individual is unique. There are two reasons for this. Most of us have a unique set of **genes**. These are the factors that control our inheritance. Nearly all living things have a set of genes that is different from every other individual. The second reason is that we all have different experiences. Even identical twins will eat differently and so develop slightly differently.

A class of pupils

Cats are not dogs!

Although all cats are different, we know they are not dogs! This means that they must also have something in common. Look at the comparison between cats and dogs.

	Cats	Dogs
claws that can draw in	✓	✗
whiskers wider than head	✓	✗
short muzzle	✓	✗

Sets of common features allow you to tell one type of **organism** from another. Each type of organism is called a **species**. All members of a species can interbreed.

1. Give two reasons why each living organism ends up slightly different from every other organism.
2. What are genes?
3. Give an example where two organisms have exactly the same genes.
4. Explain what is meant by a species.
5. Why do you think cats' whiskers are wider than their heads?

Vive la différence!   4.02

Can you roll your tongue? You either can, or cannot. There is no in-between and you cannot learn it. It is like leg number. There are 6 in insects and 8 in spiders (barring accidents). This is **discontinuous variation.**

All living things are different. Biologists want to measure the differences to help understand variation in species. When we come to measure differences we find two patterns of variation. The first we have seen in tongue rolling.

The second pattern is the one we get if we measure height or hand spans in people. In these cases we find a whole range of measures from the smallest to the biggest. Any height between 0.57 m (the shortest person in the 1997 *Guinness Book of Records*) and 2.36 m (the tallest person in the 1997 *Guinness Book of Records*) is possible. This is **continuous variation.**

The way we present information about variation helps us understand the patterns. We show discontinuous variation on a bar chart. Each type of variation is distinct. It is given its own bar on the graph. There are no in-between types.

Continuous variation should be shown on a **line graph.** This is because any of the in-between measures is possible. You will only have measured a sample. Sometimes you may want to divide continuous data into clumps. For example you may count the numbers of people in a certain height range. This is useful when you only have small numbers in a sample. If you do this then you can show each clump as a bar on a bar chart. The bar chart shows height data for a class plotted as clumps on a bar chart.

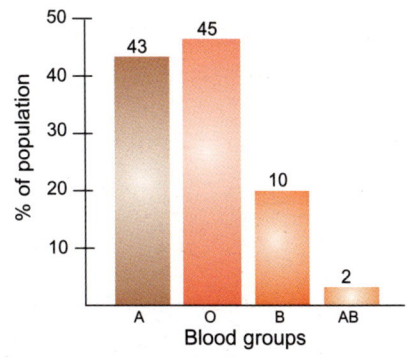

Each blood group is distinct

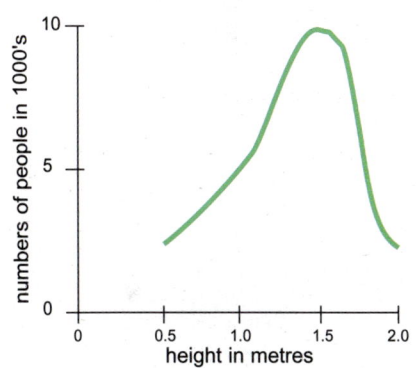

Line graphs show continuous variation patterns

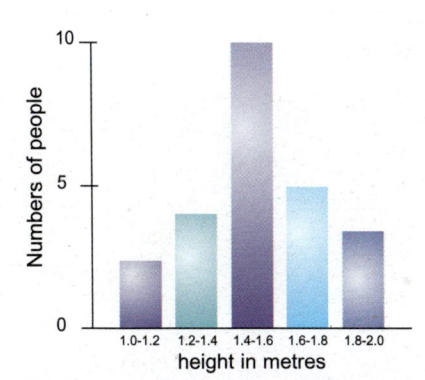

You can clump continuous data and use a bar chart

---

1 Eyes come in particular colours. Feet can be all sorts of sizes. What sort of variation is each?

2 What is the difference between continuous and discontinuous variation?

3 Which of the following show continuous variation? Explain your choice.

   a Hair colour

   b Finger length

   c Weight

   d Presence or absence of ear lobes

   e Speed at the 100 m race

   f Ability to do maths tests

4 Describe the shape of the line graph for height. Why might all features with continuous variation have this shape?

Finding out: Looking at variation

Variation in cubit length

The easiest way to get some idea of variation within a species is to measure yourself. You could do this in your class or year group. Before measures were standardized, people used parts of the body as units (we still measure horses in hands, the width of a palm). A cubit was the length of the arm from the elbow to the tip of the middle finger.

Instructions

1 Measure the cubit length of everyone in the class. Use a metre rule along the outside edge of the arm.

2 For each person measure each arm separately. Only measure to the nearest whole centimetre.

3 Arrange the measures in order. Take the shortest from the longest to find the range of measurement in the group. Divide the range into five equal lengths. Count the number of people in each section of the range and plot a graph of this.

4 Plot separate graphs for right and left arms.

5 What shape is the graph?

6 Are there any differences between the right and left arm patterns and the overall pattern?

7 Are there any differences between right- and left-handed people? (You may need to collect more data from other groups before you can answer this question.)

Measuring a cubit

Variation in fingerprints

Another piece of variation that is very specific to people is their fingerprint pattern.

Instructions

1 After a demonstration by your teacher use an ink pad to make a set of your own fingerprints.

2 Collate the class data about how many of each type of pattern there are.

3 Draw a bar graph of your data.

4 Are there any differences between boys and girls?

5 Do particular fingers have one of the patterns more often than the others?

6 What possible reason could there be for different fingerprint patterns?

The main types of fingerprint — arch, loop, whorl

Sorting out millions

4.03

There are over one million sorts of living thing. Each of these is a **species.** New species are being found each week. Biologists hope to study all of these, as well as extinct species like dinosaurs. How will they cope?

Classification

If you go to a library you will find the books arranged in sections. Works of fiction are in alphabetical order by author. Romantic fiction is on a separate shelf. This grouping of books makes it easier to find what you want. In just the same way, biologists group species to make them easier to study. People have always done this. In the past it was important to know things like which plants are poisonous and which animals are likely to attack you.

Grouping living things

Imagine you are visiting a new planet. How will you group the living things you find there? You have to decide which features are important. Biologists have had to decide how to group the species found here on Earth.

Biologists believe that all living things are related. They think that life is **evolving.** This means that over many, many generations living things change. Old species turn into new species over millions of years. If this is true related organisms will have features in common. You can expect them to share a body plan or ways of doing things in their bodies. For example a rat and a cow are both mammals. They are both hairy and make milk to feed their young.

So biologists try to group living things on the basis of how similar they are. They are trying to show the relationships between species.

These are both mammals

Did You Know?

The General Sherman tree is the biggest living thing in the world. It weighs 6100 tonnes and would make 5 000 000 000 matches

1. What is a species?
2. What does it mean to say that organisms are evolving?
3. Give two reasons why biologists group living things.
4. Look at the photographs of the wasp, the spider and the ant on the right. Biologists think two of these are closely related. Just by looking at the outside, which would you put in the same group and why?

4.04 Kingdoms of life

Biologists believe that all living things started from a single cell. So all living things are relatives, (fortunately some relatives are rather distant!). Living things survive in very different ways. We call the groups showing these different ways of living, **kingdoms.** A kingdom is a group of organisms with a special approach to life. Within each kingdom are other groups which have a common body plan. These groups are called **phyla** (singular **phylum**). There are at least four main kingdoms.

Euglena moves and makes its own food

Protists
Protists are single-celled organisms. They include a wide range of living things. Some single cells, like *Amoeba*, are animal-like. Others, like *Pleurococcus*, are plant-like. Some, like *Euglena*, are in-between. The first living things would have been single cells. Some protists look like plant cells and others like animals or fungi. This suggests that single cells could evolve into other groups.

The green powder on the tree trunk is a colony of Pleurococcus

Plants
Plants are multi-celled organisms that make their own food. They have chlorophyll in some of their cells. Being able to make their own food means they do not need to move about in search of food.

Animals
Animals are multi-cellular organisms with nerves and muscles. They eat other living things. Because they cannot make food they need to be able to move about to find food. To enable them to move above, they have to have muscles. To 'see' where they are going they need complex senses. For these senses they need nerves.

Fungi
Fungi are generally made of threads without proper cells. They eat their food by dissolving it outside them and then sucking up the juices.

Which kingdom?
Living things rarely fall neatly into groups. So there will be some organisms which do not fit neatly into any of these four groups.

Moulds are very good at cleaning up dead bodies

---

1 In your own words say what a kingdom is.

2 List the most important features of each of the four main kingdoms. Explain why they are the most important.

3 Sponges are organisms which only have two sorts of cell. They do not have organs like other multi-cellular creatures. They do not move about. They do not make their own food. Their feeding cells are like an *Amoeba*. Which kingdom would you put them in? Explain why.

(Remember there are no absolute right answers!)

Plant body plans

4.05

Within the plant kingdom are the following groups, called **phyla** (singular **phylum**) which have common body plans:

Plant phyla

- **Algae** are plants like seaweeds which are made from a sheet of similar cells called a frond. They have only a few special cells. They have hardly any organs. They could have evolved from protists which grew together as a colony. Algae use spores to reproduce.

- **Mosses** are the first plants to have grown on land. They have leaves one cell thick and a simple stem. They have rootlets made from only a few cells. They need to live in damp conditions. Mosses use spores to reproduce.

- **Ferns** are the first group with a main transport system. This is made from phloem and xylem cells. They have a stem, leaves and multicellular roots. Because of their development they can live in dry as well as damp conditions. Ferns use spores to reproduce.

- **Seed plants** is the final plant phylum. They use seeds for reproduction. There are two groups. The first is gymnosperms such as conifers. Their seeds are open to the air during development. The second group is flowering plants. They have seeds which are always enclosed during development. Many seed plants are woody and grow into bushes and tall trees. The most advanced seed plants are herbs like grasses.

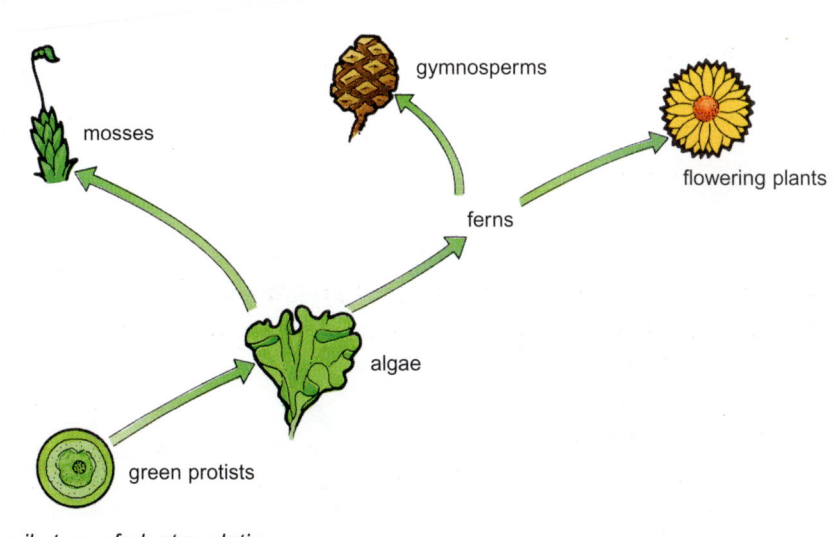

Family tree of plant evolution

The sea lettuce is a simple alga

Bracken's roots and transport system enable it to live in dry places

Even some trees are flowering plants (horse-chestnut)

Did You Know?

Some algae live at depths of over 250 m where more than 99% of the light has been filtered out.

1. Name the most important feature of each plant phylum. Why do you think this is the most important?
2. How might simple plants have evolved?
3. How are ferns different from algae?

4.06 Animal body plans

Animals are all related to each other. We can trace their evolution from simple animals to more complex ones. Within the animal kingdom are the following groups, called **phyla** (singular **phylum**):

Animal phyla

- **Jellyfish** are the simplest animals. They have only two cell layers but still manage to produce nerves and muscles.

- **Segmented worms** (such as earthworms) are made from many similar sections. They have three cell layers and a nerve cord along the belly.

- **Arthropods** also have segments. They have a hard outer skeleton and legs. The biggest group is the insects. These have three body sections and six legs. The group also includes centipedes, crabs and spiders.

- **Molluscs** are unsegmented and often have a shell made from calcium. They have a muscular foot. They include snails, slugs, octopuses and squid. Although they do not have segments they are closely related to arthropods. Their young grow in a similar way to start with.

- **Chordates** have a nerve cord along the back. Most of them are vertebrates. This means they have bones. There are five groups of vertebrates. Fish have scales, gills and fins to help them live in water. Amphibians have a damp skin and young called tadpoles. Reptiles have scales but use lungs for breathing. They lay soft shelled eggs. Birds have feathers and wings. They lay hard-shelled eggs. Mammals are hairy and suckle their young on milk. People are mammals.

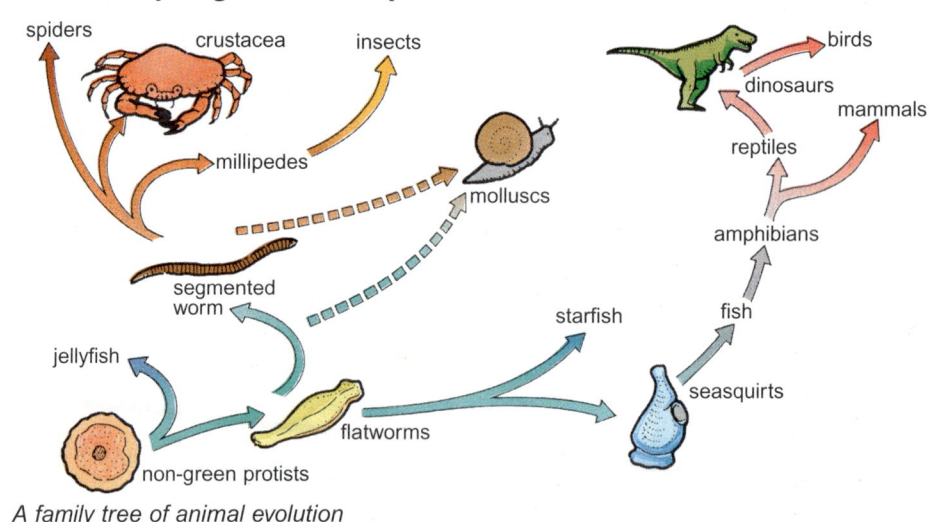

Over three quarters of all insects are beetles

The octopus is the most intelligent invertebrate

A typical vertebrate

Did You Know?
The longest earthworm was 6.7 m!

A family tree of animal evolution

1. Describe a key feature of the simplest animals.
2. What is special about arthropods compared to segmented worms?
3. Describe the differences between the five types of vertebrate.
4. How can you tell that people are chordates?

60

A biologist's solution

Everything has a name

All living things are classified by biologists to help us to understand them. Putting them in groups links them with other related species. An eighteenth-century Swedish biologist called Carl von Linné (or Linnaeus) was the first person to really organize a system for grouping organisms. He established the basis of the system still used today to classify every species. Each species is given a two-part name (a bit like ourselves) but written with the surname first. The surname (**genus**) tells us which other organisms it is related to. Then there is a species name which can be chosen by the first biologist to name it.

Similar **genera** (plural) are put into **families**. Similar families are put into **orders** and these are grouped into **classes**. The classes make up the phyla we described in the previous section. Groups of these phyla in turn make up the kingdoms. The whole thing works like a library classification. The picture on the right shows how the classification system works.

Look at the example of the common domestic cat (*Felis domestica*) below:

Carl von Linné invented the Linnaean system of classification

domestica	species name	– means domesticated
Felis	genus name	– all small cats including the serval
Felidae	family name	– all cats including lions and tigers
Carnivora	order name	– all carnivorous mammals including dogs and weasels
Mammals	class name	– furry warm-blooded animals, suckle their young on milk
Chordate	phylum name	– animals with dorsal nerve cord and a tail
Animal	kingdom name	– organisms with nerves and muscles

The same can be done for plants. The example is for the daisies that grow in lawns.

perrenis	comes up every year
Bellis	daisy-like plants
Compositae	plants with similar flowers like dandelions
Asterales	plants with star-like flowers
Angiosperm	plants with enclosed seeds
Spermatophyte	plants with seeds
Plants	multicellular organisms that photosynthesize

Library = ALL LIVING THINGS
Adult library = KINGDOM
Non-fiction = PHYLUM
Biology = ORDER
science = CLASS
animals = FAMILY
Birds = GENUS
single book = SPECIES

1 The lion is a big cat. Its biological name is *Panthera leo*. Write out the complete biological description of the lion.

2 Find out what groups human beings belong to and explain why we are placed in each.

4.08 The key to life

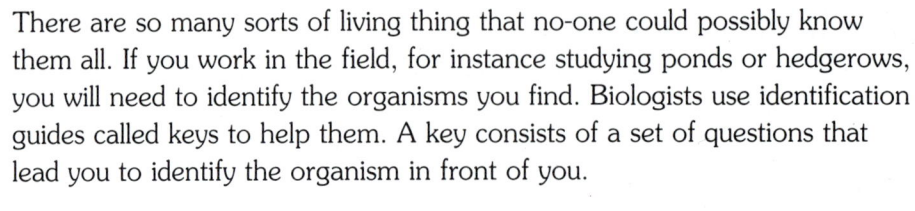

There are so many sorts of living thing that no-one could possibly know them all. If you work in the field, for instance studying ponds or hedgerows, you will need to identify the organisms you find. Biologists use identification guides called keys to help them. A key consists of a set of questions that lead you to identify the organism in front of you.

Consider this key for identifying the big cats.

1.	Is the cat striped?	Yes	It is a tiger
		No	Go to Q2
2.	Is the cat spotted?	Yes	Go to Q3
		No	Go to Q5
3.	Do the claws retract?	Yes	Go to Q4
		No	It is a cheetah
4.	Are you in Africa?	Yes	It is a leopard
		No	It is a jaguar
5.	Does the male have a mane?	Yes	It is a lion
		No	It is a puma

This is fine as far as it goes. However, if you had only a lion cub in front of you, you would get it wrong (they have spots)! Suppose you only have a lioness; you could not answer question 5. You might also get question 4 wrong if you were in an African zoo where they kept jaguars.

As you can see, writing a clear and unambiguous key is not easy. You need to ask questions that can be answered with only one specimen in front of you. The questions need to apply to any member of the species. Questions should be straightforward, requiring a yes or no answer.

As a key maker you need to try to divide the groups you are working on into those with and without an obvious feature (e.g. coat pattern), and then to subdivide these groups using some other feature.

① Revise the key for big cats to eliminate the problems identified.

② Using the plant leaves in the pictures make your own key for someone else to use. Get them to try it out!

③ Devise your own key and use it to identify insects collected from your school grounds. How easy was it to use? Did it work for all your insect examples or did you have to make modifications to your key?

Pure substances

CHAPTER 5

5.01

SEPARATING MIXTURES

What is a pure substance?
Have you ever looked at the list of ingredients on packets and tins of food? The ingredients are the things used to make the food. They are listed in order on the label: the one which is present in the largest amounts is first, the second largest second and so on.

Here are lists of ingredients for two packets from the kitchen cupboard. The ingredient present in largest amounts in Packet 1 is starch. (In case you haven't guessed, Packet 1 is chicken noodle soup.)

Packet 1	Packet 2
Starch, maltodextrin, salt, yeast, wheatflour, yeast extract, flavourings, colourings, vegetable oil, dried chicken, chicken fat, onion powder, lactic acid, spice, herb extracts.	Sodium hydrogencarbonate

You will notice that Packet 2 is different from Packet 1 in one very important way. It contains only one substance. This substance is sodium hydrogencarbonate (sometimes called bicarbonate of soda). When you buy Packet 2 you are buying a **pure substance**. A pure substance contains no **impurities**.

> **Did You Know?**
> A pure substance has an exact melting-point. Impure substances melt over a range of temperature.

1 Why do you think a pure substance will cost more than an impure substance?

2 Part of a catalogue page from a firm selling chemicals is shown on the right.

   LR = laboratory reagent
   AR = analytical reagent

   a Which form is cheapest to buy and which most expensive?

   b What is the meaning of the word 'assay'?

   c Name two impurities in LR calcium carbonate which are not present in AR calcium carbonate.

   d Why is it unlikely that calcium chloride crystals are made from calcium metal?

3 At the end of an experiment Tim had some pure AR calcium carbonate left. Why is it unwise for him to put it back in the bottle?

Calcium metal, granules
25 g	£2.75
100 g	£4.25
200 g	£7.50

Ca
Contact with water liberates highly flammable gas

Calcium carbonate,
(Marble chippings)
Approx. 13mm (irregular)
(Calcium carbonate ore)
1 kg	£2.06
3 kg	£3.70

Calcium carbonate, LR (powder)
1 kg	£2.16
3 kg	£4.40

$CaCO_3$
Assay, min. 98.5% (on dried)
Maxium limits of impurities
Acid insoluble	0.05%
Arsenic (As)	0.0004%
Chloride (Cl)	0.05%
Iron (Fe)	0.02%
Lead (Pb)	0.002%
Loss on drying (105 °C)	1%
Sulphate (SO_4)	0.25%

Calcium carbonate, AR (powder)
250 g	£4.60
500 g	£7.05

$CaCO_3$
Assay, min. 99.5%
Ammonia (NH_3)	<0.1%
Barium and strontium (Ba)	<0.04%
Chloride (Cl)	<0.001%
Heavy metals (Pb)	<0.001%
Iron (Fe)	<0.001%
Magnesium (Mg)	<0.01%
Nitrate (NO_3)	<0.01%
Phosphate (PO_4)	<0.001%
Potassium (K)	<0.01%
Silicate (SiO_2)	<0.01%
Sodium (Na)	<0.02%
Soluble alkali	<0.25 milli equivs%
Sulphate (SO_4)	<0.005%

Calcium carbonate, Iceland spar
25 g	£2.85

63

5.02 Pure salt from rock salt

Pure salt is made from rock salt found in the ground. Rock salt is a mixture of salt and other rocks including sandstone.

Purifying rock salt

You may have carried out an experiment to make some pure salt from some crushed rock salt. This experiment involves three stages:

(1) Adding the crushed rock salt to water and stirring.

(2) Filtering the mixture.

(3) Heating the solution to form solid salt.

In hot countries salt is produced by evaporation of sea water. The sun provides the energy to evaporate the water.

Rock salt is impure

Did You Know?

Rock salt deposits are found in places which were once large seas. Evaporation of water left these deposits. Much of England was once under the sea.

Rock salt is mined underground

Large, shallow pans are used when evaporating sea water

1. Copy the three diagrams and label them using words from this list.

   beaker   filter funnel   filter paper   evaporating basin   gauze
   residue   salt solution   stirring rod   tripod   Bunsen burner

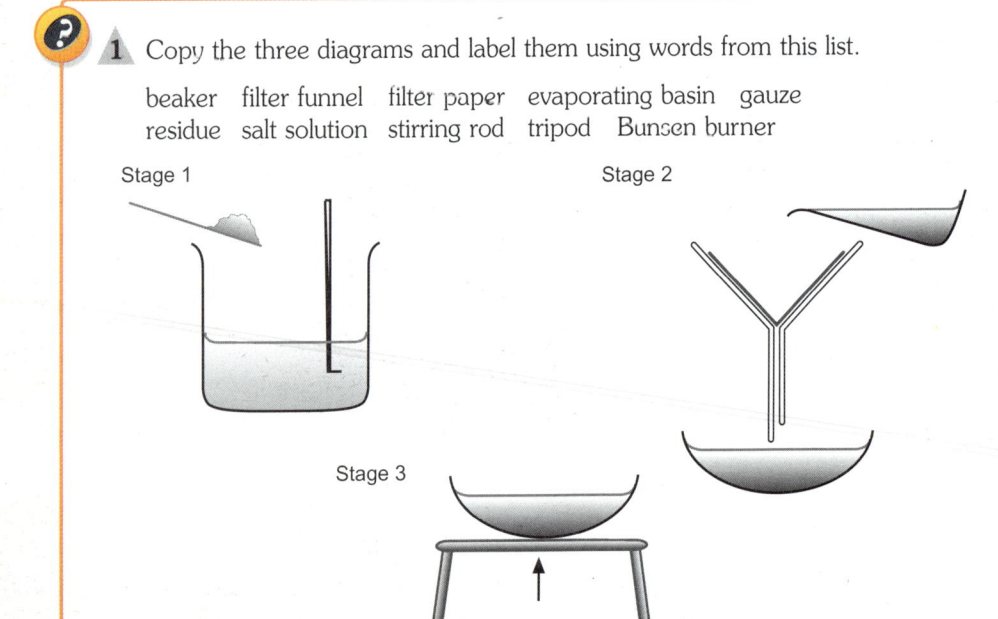

   Stage 1
   Stage 2
   Stage 3

   The three Stages in purifying rock salt

2. a Why is the mixture stirred in Stage 1 of the experiment?

   b What is dissolved in Stage 1?

   c What does the solution look like when it drips from the funnel in Stage 2?

   d What possible dangers are there when carrying out Stage 3?

3. Why do we not produce salt by evaporation of sea water in Great Britain?

4. When salt is produced from seawater, why are big, shallow pans used rather than smaller, deep ones?

5. What is rock salt used for in Winter?

Finding out: Purification of rock salt

Rock salt is sodium chloride mixed with insoluble impurities. In this experiment you will remove these impurities to produce pure sodium chloride.

Instructions

1 Put about 40 cm^3 of distilled water into the small beaker. Add 3 spatula measures of crushed rock salt to this. Stir with the glass rod until the salt has dissolved. The impurities will remain undissolved.

2 Take a piece of filter paper and fold it in half and in half again as shown in the diagram below. Open it out to produce a paper cone with three thicknesses of paper on one side and one on the other. Put this cone into the filter funnel and moisten the paper cone with a few drops of water to fix the cone inside the funnel.

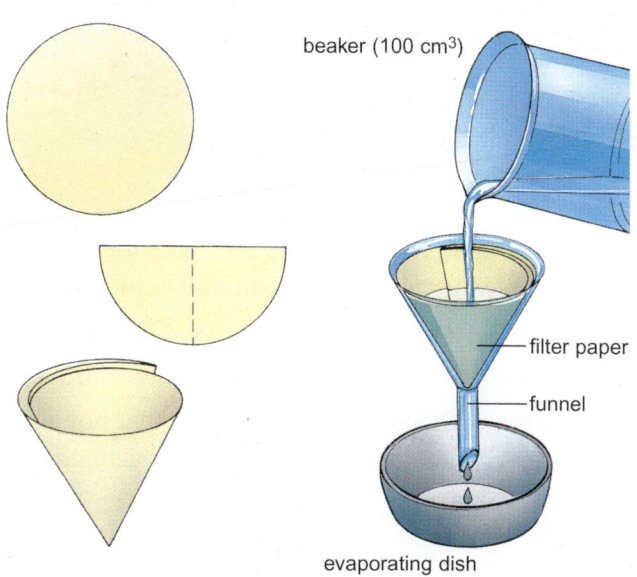

3 Pour the solution from the beaker into the funnel and collect the solution which passes through the filter paper in the evaporating basin.

WARNING

You must wear goggles when evaporating this solution. The solution can spit. If spitting occurs, turn down the gas to make the flame smaller.

4 Place the evaporating basin on the tripod and gauze and heat steadily until the solution starts to spit.

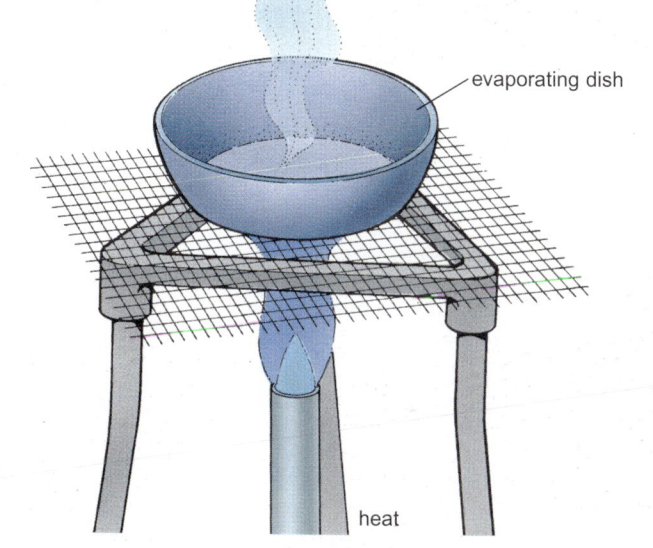

5 Then, evaporate the solution more slowly using the apparatus shown below.

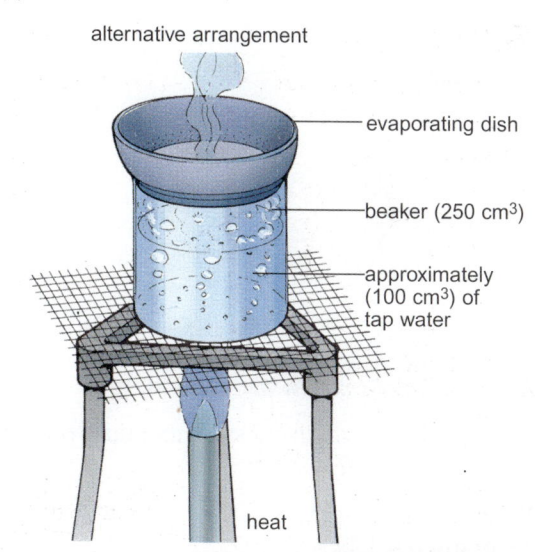

6 When the salt appears dry, leave the evaporating basin to cool. You will have produced some white crystals of salt.

5.03 Pure water from sea water

Did You Know?

In Abu Dhabi, in the Middle East, one factory can produce nine million litres of pure water a day from sea water. Producing large amounts of water has turned areas of desert in Saudi Arabia into farmland. In Israel orange trees are growing on land which was once desert.

We have seen that in hot countries salt can be made from sea water. It is also possible to make pure water (or drinking water) from sea water.

Making pure water in the laboratory

The diagram below shows apparatus which can be used in the laboratory to produce some pure water from some blue ink.

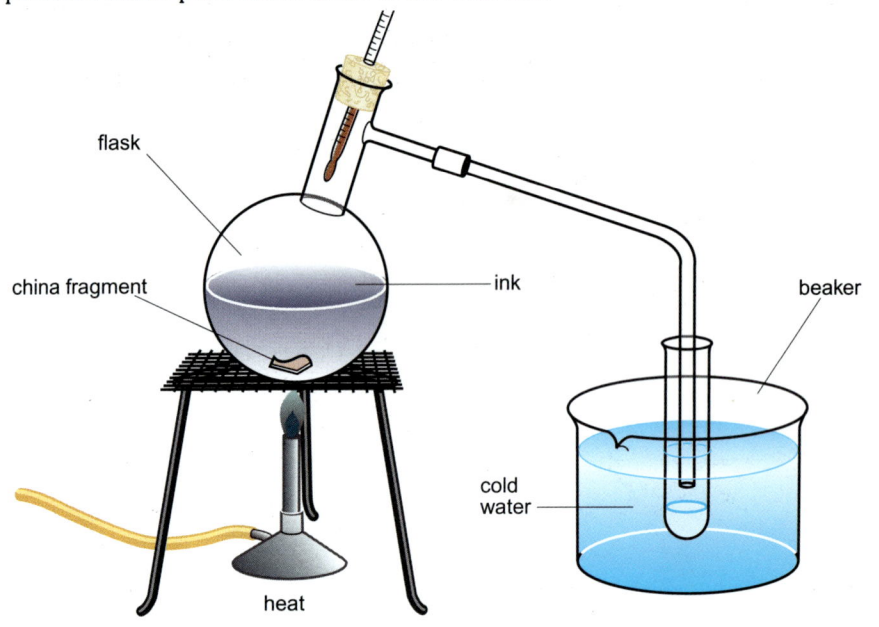

The ink in the flask is heated gently until it boils.

When the steam leaves the flask and enters the test tube, it is cooled down and is collected as pure water (called the **distillate**) in the test tube.

Pure water has been produced from ink by a process of **distillation**. This involves two processes together – **boiling** followed by **condensing**.

If you have watched this experiment you will have seen that not all the steam is condensed to water. Some of it escapes. It is not a very efficient way of carrying out this distillation.

1. What colour steam will be produced?
2. What will be the highest temperature on the thermometer?
3. What name is given to the pure water that collects in the test tube?
4. Can you think of any uses for the pure water collected?
5. Of the two processes boiling and condensing, one needs energy to take place and the other gives out energy. Which process needs energy and which gives out energy?
6. Why does hot steam produce a more serious burn than boiling water?

Further distillation

5.04

Distillation involves **boiling** followed by **condensing.** If the process is to be efficient no energy is wasted; no uncondensed steam should escape.

The diagram below shows apparatus which can be used for distillation. The steam passes through a **condenser.** This consists of a tube through which the steam passes and a cooling jacket. Cold water passes through this cooling jacket. The water cools the steam and condenses it. The energy given out when the steam condenses is taken away by the cold water. This type of condenser is sometimes called a Liebig condenser after Baron Justus von Liebig.

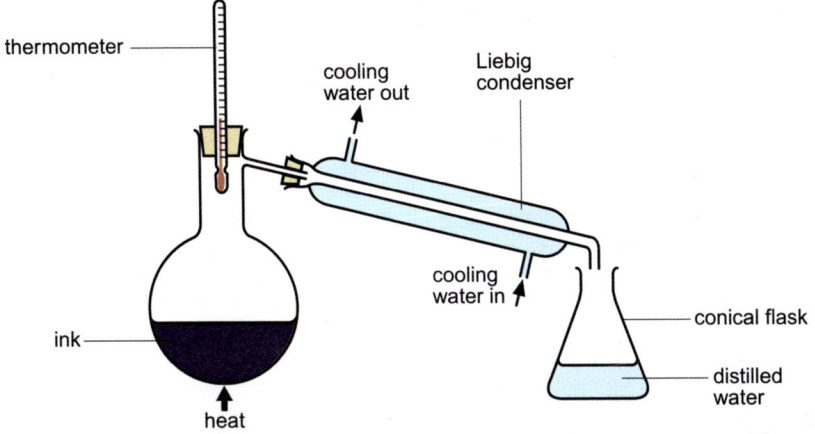

> **Did You Know?**
>
> Liebig was a famous chemist about one hundred and fifty years ago. He discovered several new chemicals including chloroform. This came to be used as an anaesthetic for surgical operations. He did not invent the condenser – somebody else did this but Liebig made it popular by showing how it could be used.

Distillation using a Liebig condenser

1 Why would this apparatus not be suitable for distillation?

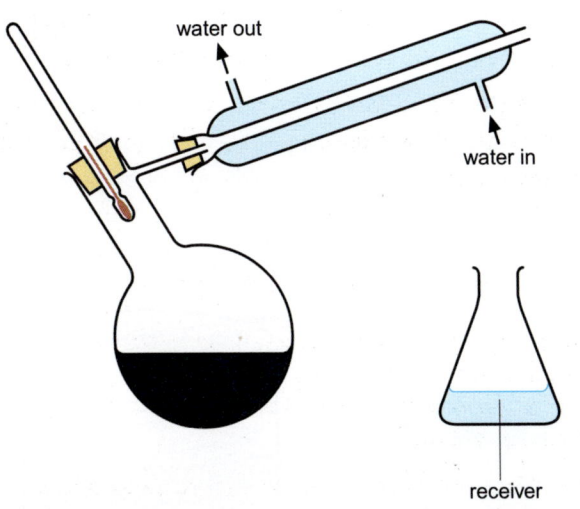

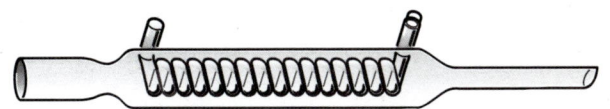

A Graham condenser

3 The diagram shows a still used to make distilled water in a school laboratory. Write a few sentences explaining how it works.

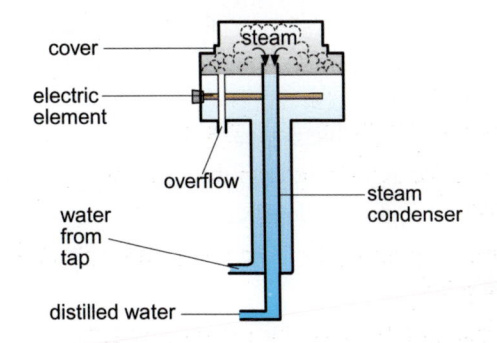

A laboratory still

2 What is there about the design of a Graham condenser that makes it more efficient than a Liebig condenser?

5.05 Mixing liquids

Miscible and immiscible liquids

Some liquids mix together well. For example, beer contains two liquids – water and ethanol. These two liquids mix thoroughly so that the beer has the same composition throughout. Liquids that mix together completely are called **miscible** liquids.

Some pairs of liquids do not mix. For example, when oil and water are put into the same beaker, they form two separate layers. The oil layer floats on the water layer because oil is less dense than water. Pairs of liquids that do not mix are called **immiscible** liquids. The lower layer contains the liquid with the greater density.

Separating miscible and immiscible liquids

Separating miscible liquids (such as ethanol and water) is difficult to do and requires **fractional distillation**.

Separating immiscible liquids is easier. It can be done using a tap funnel. Look at the diagram below. The two liquids are put into the tap funnel. The tap in the bottom of the funnel is opened and the first liquid is run into the beaker. The tap is closed. The beaker is changed and the second liquid is run into the new beaker.

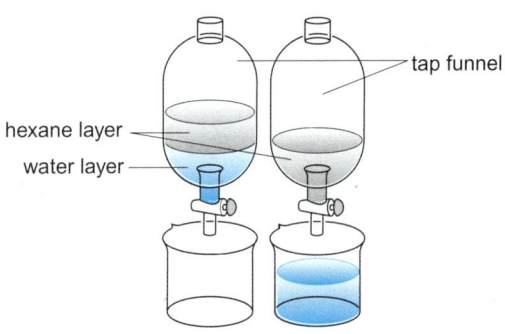

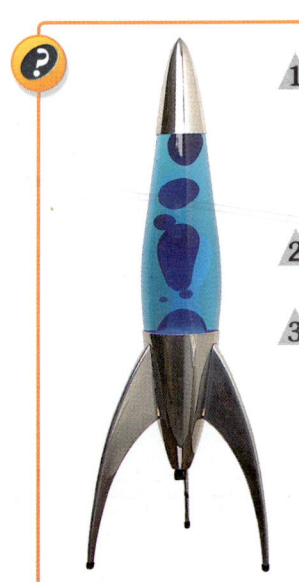

Did You Know?

When oil and water are shaken together an emulsion is formed as they do not completely mix. Adding a detergent enables oil and water to mix. This is why detergents are used to remove oil from sea birds after an oil spillage.

1. A lava lamp contains two immiscible liquids. As you watch it you see bubbles of one liquid moving upward through the other. Why does this happen?

2. Can you name some pairs of miscible liquids?

3. Which liquid, oil or water, has the greater density?

4. The diagram below shows two beakers. One contains a pair of miscible liquids and one contains a pair of immiscible liquids. Which is which?

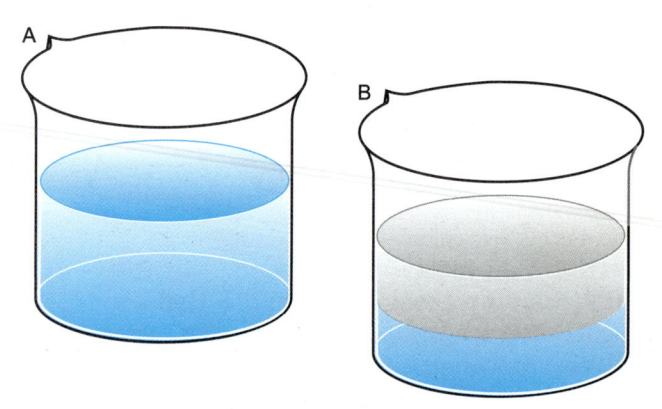

68

Separating ethanol and water

5.06

Ethanol and water are a pair of miscible liquids. Miscible liquids can usually be separated by the process of **fractional distillation**.

The apparatus shown below is used to separate liquids by fractional distillation. The process relies on the fact that different liquids have different boiling points. The boiling point of ethanol is 78 °C and the boiling point of water is 100 °C.

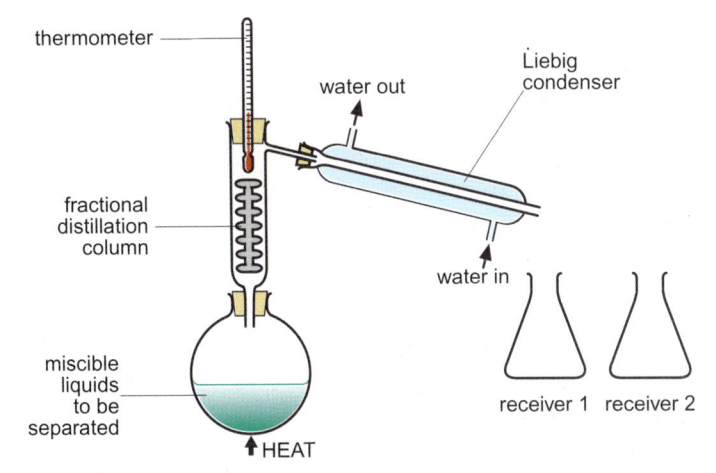

Apparatus used for fractional distillation

The mixture of ethanol and water is put into the flask with a few pieces of broken china. The broken china helps to ensure smooth boiling. The flask is heated gently with receiver 1 in place. When the temperature on the thermometer reads 78 °C, the ethanol boils and the vapour passes through the condenser and the ethanol liquid collects in receiver 1. This is called **fraction** 1. Any water vapour produced condenses in the column and drips back into the flask. When all of the ethanol has gone, the temperature on the thermometer rises and receiver 2 is put in place. At 100 °C water distils over and is collected in receiver 2. This is fraction 2.

Did You Know?

The tax charged on alcoholic drinks is based on their strength. Hundreds of years ago tax collectors used gun powder to test the strength of a drink. They put some of the alcoholic drink on a small pile of gunpowder and tried to set light to it. If the gunpowder burned the solution was 100% proof. (Note – this is not 100% alcohol.)

Did You Know?

Air can be separated into oxygen and nitrogen. First air has to be cooled and turned into liquid air. This is then allowed to warm up. Liquid oxygen has a boiling point of –183 °C and liquid nitrogen has a boiling point of –196 °C.

---

1 Distillation can be used to separate a liquid from a solution e.g. water from sea water. It uses two separate processes, b_____ and c_____. What are these two processes?

2 Which has the lower boiling point ethanol or water?

3 Ali is given some apparatus plus a Bunsen burner, cork, glass tubing and clamps he needs to hold it. Draw a diagram to show how he could use the apparatus to separate two liquids by fractional distillation.

4 Why is it difficult to separate two liquids with boiling points 110 °C and 115 °C?

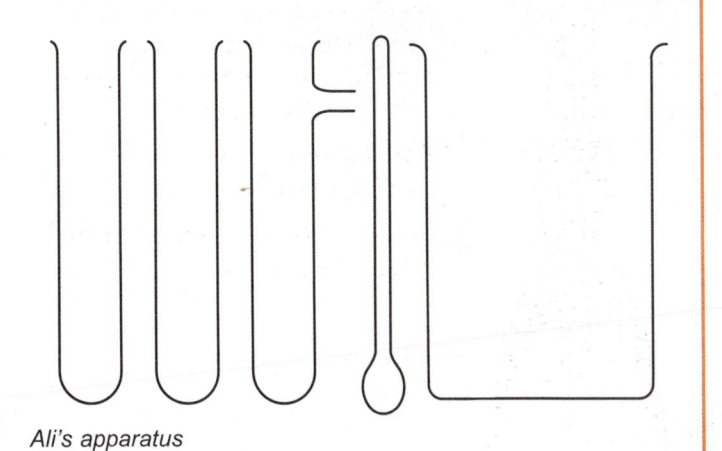

Ali's apparatus

5.07 Uses of fractional distillation

Fractional distillation can be used to separate mixtures of miscible liquids. Fractional distillation is used in industry to produce useful materials.

Spirit	Source
whisky	barley, rye or maize
rum	molasses (syrup made from sugar cane refining)
brandy	grapes
gin	grain flavoured with juniper berries

Whisky making

Whisky is a spirit made by fractional distillation of a mixture of ethanol and water.

Whisky is made in a factory called a **distillery**. First of all barley is malted by soaking it in water, allowing the seeds to germinate and then drying in a peat-fired oven. The peat smoke gives much of the flavour to the whisky.

The mixture is then ground into a fine powder called malt. This is mixed with warm water to produce a sugary solution called 'wort'. Yeast is added and **fermentation** takes place. This turns the sugars in the solution into ethanol.

The resulting mixture of ethanol and water is then distilled twice in copper fractional distillation vessels called **stills**.

At this point the liquid does not taste much like whisky. The concentrated ethanol solution produced is stored in oak casks for years to mature. During this process the whisky absorbs colouring and flavouring from the casks.

Whisky is distilled twice during manufacture

Refining crude oil

Crude oil is a thick black liquid found in many parts of the world. As it is found it is not very useful. At one time crude oil was called pitch and was used to stop wooden ships leaking. When it was first found in Texas, farmers used to set fire to it to remove it.

Crude oil is made into saleable products by fractional distillation. This is sometimes called **refining** and takes place in a **refinery**. You will notice it contains a lot of columns and miles of pipes.

Fractional distillation produces different fractions. Each fraction has its own range of boiling point and its own uses. These fractions include petrol, kerosene (used for fuel for jet engines), diesel oil, fuel oils etc. No part of the crude oil is unused. Even the tarry mass which does not distil over is used. It is called bitumen.

Oil is refined by fractional distillation

---

1. Distilleries are built in areas where there are farms. The remains of the malt is removed from the solution but it is not wasted. Suggest how this material is used.
2. Why are old sherry casks used for maturing whisky rather than new ones?
3. Why are oil refineries built close to the sea?
4. What is bitumen used for?

Separating dyes

5.08

Inks are mixtures of dyes dissolved in a solvent, usually water.

You can do an experiment to show different dyes that make the ink. First of all you put a drop of ink onto the centre of a piece of filter paper using a teat pipette. You then allow the blot to dry. Next you drop drops of water onto the centre of the ink blot using a teat pipette. If you do this carefully the ink blot gets larger. The different dyes spread out at different speeds. Each dye forms a separate ring.

The picture below shows the filter paper with a drop of red ink before water is dropped onto it. It also shows the filter paper after – there are two separate red rings. Each ring comes from a different dye. This ink must be made up of two dyes.

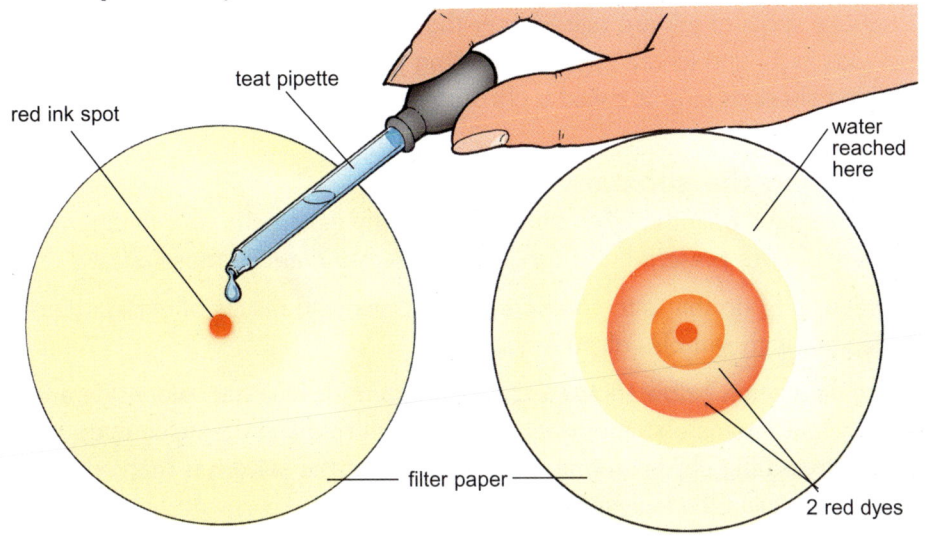

Before and after water was dropped onto the ink blot

Did You Know?

Although chromatography is simple to carry out it was not used until 1903. The Russian scientist Michel Tswett used it to separate coloured materials from plants. It was not used widely until about 1940 and has developed into one of the most important methods of separating and identifying chemicals.

This simple experiment with coloured dyes and filter paper is the basis of a very important method of separating substances called **chromatography**. This word means colour writing.

1 Another experiment was done with purple ink.

   a How many dyes were in the purple dye?

   b What colour were these dyes?

   c Look at both the illustrations.

      Do you think that the same dye was in both the red ink and the purple ink?

      What makes you think this?

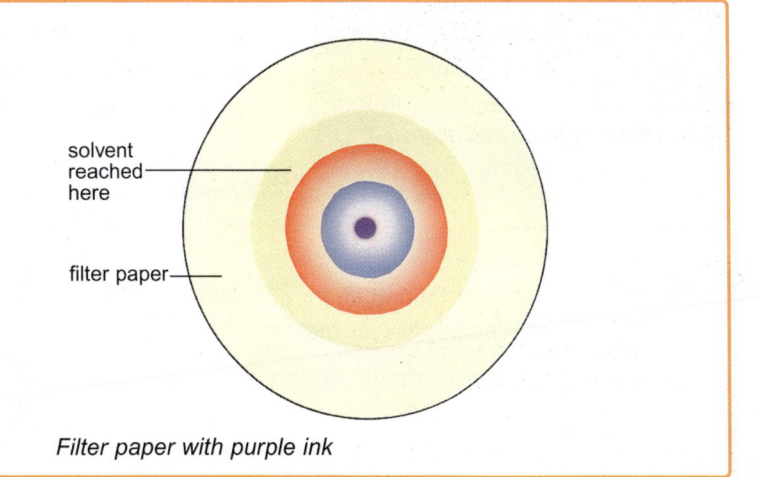

Filter paper with purple ink

71

5.09 Chromatography

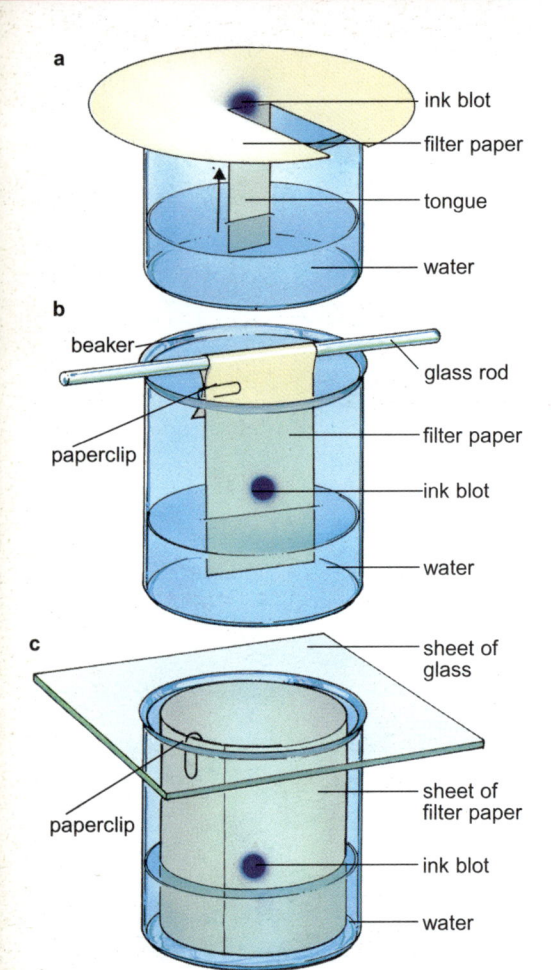

a

- ink blot
- filter paper
- tongue
- water

b

- beaker
- glass rod
- paperclip
- filter paper
- ink blot
- water

c

- sheet of glass
- paperclip
- sheet of filter paper
- ink blot
- water

Three methods of carrying out chromatography

Did You Know?

Paper chromatography is only one method of chromatography. Gas-liquid chromatography is a very important method. It can be used to identify very complex mixtures such as the ingredients in a perfume.

Better methods for chromatography

You need a very steady hand when enlarging a blot with water from a teat pipette. There are better ways of doing this. Three possible methods are shown in the diagram on the left.

In (a) the filter paper is still used but a small 'tongue' is cut out. This dips into the water in a beaker. The water slowly rises up the 'tongue', reaches the blot and spreads out as before. It produces coloured rings as before, but using this method only the right amount of water is used.

In (b) and (c) the separation of dyes takes place on a strip or sheet of filter paper. In both cases, the water moves upwards and the dyes separate to form spots on the filter paper. Each dye present forms a separate spot. A spot or spots of ink are placed near the bottom of the strip or sheet. The methods in (b) and (c) are called **ascending paper chromatography**. The resulting sheet or strip is called a **chromatogram**.

Identifying the substances present

So far we have only thought of chromatography as a method of finding the *number* of dyes present but it can also be used to *identify* those dyes.

One way to do this is to compare your results with results of experiments carried out with samples of pure dyes.

The illustration below shows a chromatogram for blue ink. Alongside are the chromatograms obtained using pale blue, purple and dark blue dyes. Before drying the chromatograms the position of the solvent is marked. This line is called the 'solvent front'.

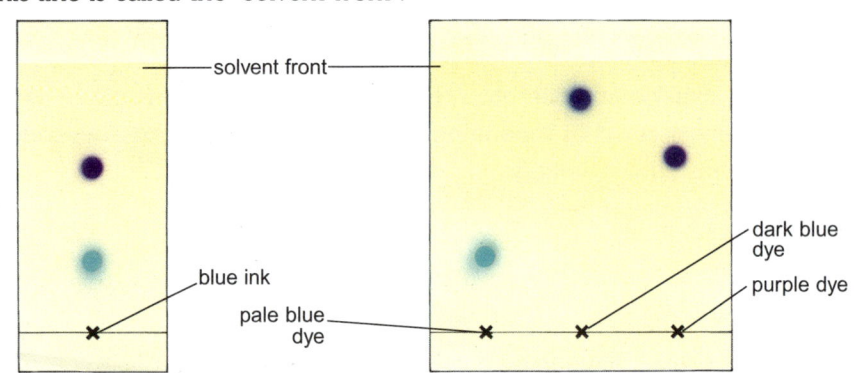

- solvent front
- blue ink
- pale blue dye
- dark blue dye
- purple dye

Chromatograms for blue ink and pale blue, dark blue and purple dyes

---

1. Why are methods (b) and (c) for chromatography called ascending paper chromatography?
2. Why should lines be drawn on the filter paper with a pencil and not a pen?
3. What can you conclude about the dyes in the blue ink?
4. Chromatography can be used to separate colourless substances such as amino acids. How could this method be modified for colourless substances?

Finding out: Orange squash dyes

Coloured dyes are used to make food look better. You are going to remove the dyes by getting them to stick to some wool. Later you can remove the dyes from the wool and separate them by chromatography.

Instructions

1. Measure 10 cm^3 of undiluted orange squash into the boiling tube and add 10 drops of dilute ethanoic acid with the teat pipette. Put the wool into the boiling tube.

2. Put the boiling tube into the beaker of boiling water and leave for five minutes. Remove the wool with the glass rod and wash the wool thoroughly with distilled water. Empty and wash the boiling tube.

3. Return the wool to the boiling tube and add 5 cm^3 of ammonia solution. Warm the boiling tube again in the beaker of hot water.

4. Transfer the solution from the boiling tube to the watch glass and evaporate carefully until only a few drops of solution remain.

5. Draw a pencil line across the filter paper strip 1 cm from the bottom. Using the capillary tube, make a small blot (about 3 mm diameter) using the solution remaining in the watch glass. Allow the blot to dry for a few minutes.

6. Suspend the filter paper strip with the filter paper just touching the chromatography solvent. (Ensure that the small blot is not in the solvent.) Leave the apparatus until the chromatography solvent has nearly reached the paper clip. Mark the position of the solvent front at the end of the experiment with a pencil.

7. When the filter paper strip has dried, fasten it into your book.

8. How many dyes are present in the orange squash?

9. What other substances are present in the orange squash? (Refer to the contents list on the bottle.)

10. Finish these sentences by choosing the correct word:
    acidic   alkaline

    a The wool is dyed by the dyes present in orange squash when in _____ solution.

    b The dye is removed from the wool in _____ solution.

> **WARNING**
> Wear eye protection

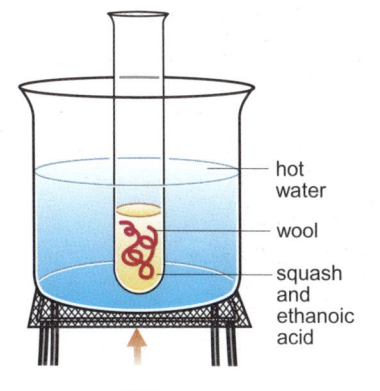

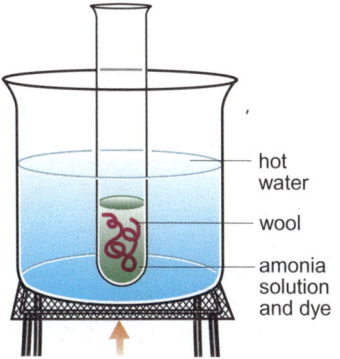

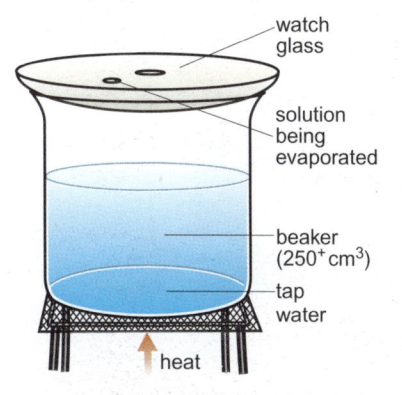

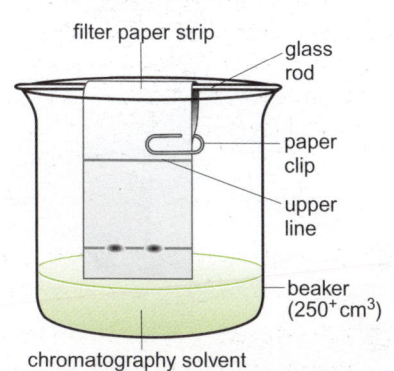

CHAPTER 6

6.01 FORCES

Pushing and pulling

Nothing can ever move without being **pulled** or **pushed**. Pushes and pulls are **forces**. Forces are needed for moving things about. They are also needed to stop things from moving about. Everything that we do involves forces. Lifting something up, walking across a floor, even sitting and standing still need forces.

The diagram below shows two important points about forces. The first point is that *a force has a direction*. The direction of a force is shown by an arrow on a diagram. The second point is that *forces involve things*. Forces are caused by things pushing or pulling other things.

The girl pulls her toy *The car pulls the caravan* *The boy pushes the lawnmower*

The upward force on the space shuttle as it leaves the launch pad is thirty million newtons (30 000 000 N).

Using a forcemeter to measure the force needed to lift a brick

Describing forces

There are two ways of describing a force. One way is to draw a diagram. You can draw an arrow on a diagram to show a force pushing or pulling something.

A second way is by writing down a phrase such as 'the man pushes the pram'. You should practise writing down descriptions of forces. Use the pattern *something* pushes or pulls *something else*. The diagrams above show you some examples.

Measuring forces

Forces are measured in **newtons** (N). You can measure the force needed to drag something or to open a door with a **forcemeter**. Lifting a brick needs a force of more than 20 N. Dragging one along the floor, usually less than 10 N.

1 Look at the diagram below. Write a description for each force shown by an arrow on the diagrams.

2 Here are some jobs done with forces.

For each one, write down whether a push or a pull is needed.

  a Opening a cupboard door
  b Closing a drawer
  c Lifting a weight off the ground

3 Draw diagrams to show the following forces.

  a A girl pulling a sledge
  b A boy pushing someone on a swing
  c A weightlifter pushing some weights above his head

Getting going

6.02

The pictures show four things that can move. All four pictures show things that are just starting to move. For something to get going, there has to be a force pushing it or pulling it.

an aircraft setting off down a runway

an arrow leaving a bow

a ball being hit by a racket

a bus setting off from a bus stop

Did You Know?

Each of the engines fitted to a jumbo jet can provide a thrust (pushing force) of one million newtons (1 000 000 N).

The string pushes the arrow

Foot pushes on ground, ground pushes on foot

Wheel pushes on road, road pushes on wheel

Look at the bow and arrow. The force that pushes the arrow comes from the bow string. As the force is pushing it from right to left, the arrow moves to the left. It is getting faster all the time that the string is pushing it.

The bus also needs a force to make it move away from the bus stop. It needs a **driving force** to push the bus in the forwards direction.

Which way?

To make something move, a force is needed. This force has to push or pull in the direction of motion. For a bus to move forwards, it needs a force in the forwards direction. Without a force in the direction of motion, a bus cannot start moving.

How do you walk? To walk forwards, you need a force to push you forwards, but when you walk your feet push backwards on the ground. Wheels on cars, bikes, trains and buses also push backwards. The forwards force comes from the ground or the track in the case of a train. It is due to **friction**, the force that stops things from sliding over each other.

If the ground is too slippery there is not enough friction so feet and wheels cannot grip. The diagram shows the forces that push us forwards when we walk or ride in a car.

1. Write down five examples of forces being used to start things moving.

   b   Write a description of each force in your five examples.

2. a   For each example that you wrote down in Q1, draw a diagram with an arrow to show the force.

3. Explain why it is not possible to walk without friction forces.

75

Finding out: Travelling downhill

Comparing speeds

You can compare the speed of cars travelling downhill by timing them over a fixed distance. The shorter the time it takes for a car to travel down the hill, the faster its speed.

Instructions

1. Prop up one end of a slope so that it is 10 cm above the ground.

2. Let go of a car from the top and time how long it takes to reach the bottom.

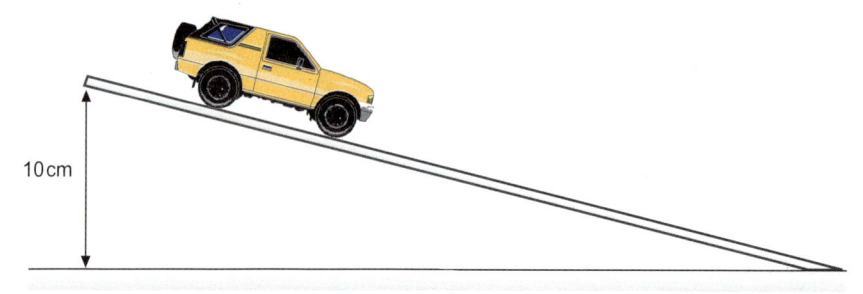

3. Repeat two or three times until you have three measured times that are close together.

4. Work out an average of these times by adding them together and dividing by three.

5. Record all your results in a table like this.

Height of slope above ground/ cm	Record of times for car to travel down slope/ s	Average time for car to travel down slope/ s
10		

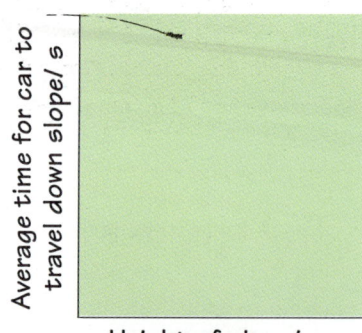

6. Carry out experiments to time the car down the slope with the slope at different heights. Use a range of heights between 10 cm and 30 cm.

7. Use the data you have collected to plot a line graph of height of slope against time taken to travel down. See if you can work out suitable scales to use.

8. Explain what your results and your graph tell you about the effect of increasing the height of the slope on the speed of the car.

Slowing down

6.03

Resistive forces

If you push something along the floor, it starts to slow down as soon as it leaves your hand. Unless you are travelling downhill, your bike starts to slow down as soon as you stop pedalling. Any method of travel on the Earth's surface or through its atmosphere needs a driving force just to keep going. This is due to the **resistive forces** that act against all moving objects.

If you swim, there is water in the space in front of you. If you walk or cycle, there is air in the way. These have to be pushed out of the way so that you can occupy the space. As well as these resistive forces from water and air, there is friction. Friction is also a resistive force that acts against two surfaces slipping or sliding over each other. You can slide easily on a polished floor or an icy surface because the friction force is low, but you cannot slide on a grass or concrete surface. The rough nature of these surfaces means that they can exert friction forces that are large enough to prevent sliding altogether.

Water resistance opposes the motion of a swimmer through water

Reducing friction

An **air-track** can be used to show how movement is easier when there is less friction. The vehicles on an air-track move like hovercraft; they are supported on a cushion of air. Push a vehicle that rests on the metal track and it only moves a few centimetres, but turn on the air supply first and it goes on … and on … and on. There is virtually no resistive force!

The Maglev train at Birmingham airport works in a similar way. It is supported above the tracks by a system of magnets that repel it upwards away from the track (not by blowing air under it as with the air track).

The skier slides over the icy surface - there is little friction

Look ... no wheels!

Did You Know?

The resistive forces that act on moving objects cause heating. Heating results in expansion. Concorde is 30 cm longer when flying at supersonic speeds than when it is on the ground.

---

1 Write down five examples of friction forces that prevent objects from slipping and sliding.

2 Imagine that you are cycling along a level road with no wind. Explain why you need to keep pedalling to carry on moving.

3 Suggest why you are able to run much faster than you can swim.

77

6.04 Forces out of balance? (1)

Changing speed
Forces are needed to start things moving. Once something is moving, other forces act to work against the motion. Few forms of transport keep going at a steady **speed.** Buses speed up as they leave the bus stop and then slow down again at traffic lights and the next bus stop. Whether a bus speeds up or slows down depends on the balance of forces acting.

Getting faster
How do you get your bike to move faster? Anyone who has ever ridden a bike knows the answer, but to understand how it happens you need to know about the forces that act on a moving bike.

First, there is the driving force that pushes forward. This is the push of the road on the wheel. Then there are resistive forces. The main one is air resistance but there are other resistive forces. A bike with flat tyres is much harder to pedal than one with the tyres blown up properly.

Your bike is harder to pedal if the tyres are not at the correct pressure.

Did You Know?
The first cars were coal-powered. Coal was burned to generate steam in a similar way to steam trains. The boiler was usually placed under the driver's seat, so driving could be hot work!

speeding up / resistive force / driving force

In order to go faster, the driving force has to be bigger than the resistive forces. So long as this is the case, the bike will speed up.

So one way to go faster is to pedal harder. This makes the wheel push on the road with a bigger force and, in turn, the road pushes back with a bigger force. Another way is to make the resistive forces smaller. Assuming that the tyres are pumped up correctly, the next thing to reduce is your profile. **Air resistance** is caused by having to push air out of the space that you want to occupy. So if you need less space, there is less air to be pushed out of the way. Cyclists reduce the resistive force by leaning forwards. With less air resistance, they can go faster.

This racing cyclist keeps a low profile to minimize the air resistance.

1 A car travels along a level road.
  a Draw the forces acting on the car when it is speeding up. Write a description of each force.
  b Draw the forces acting on the car when it is travelling at a steady speed.

2 Explain why racing cyclists often crouch over the handlebars.

3 Draw a design for a 'streamlined bike'. Explain how your design keeps resistive forces as small as possible.

78

Forces out of balance? (2)

Going steady

For a bike or a car to speed up (accelerate) the driving force has to be bigger than the resistive force. No matter how hard you pedal a bike, sooner or later you find that you cannot go any faster. This is because the resistive forces get bigger as you speed up. The diagrams below show what happens to the forces on the bike as you go faster.

going slowly ...   and faster ...   top speed

Once the resistive force is equal in size to the driving force, you no longer speed up. The bicycle maintains a steady speed. When this happens the forces are said to be **balanced**; they are equal in size and act in opposite directions. If a train or bus or car moves at a constant speed in a straight line the forces on it are balanced. It can only change speed if the forces become unbalanced. For this to happen the force acting in one direction has to become bigger than the opposing force.

Slowing down

There are several things that can cause a bike to slow down. Going uphill is one of them. If you are riding your bike on the level you can either stop pedalling, stop pedalling and apply the brakes, or just push the pedals with less force. The result of all of these is to make the resistive forces out of balance with the driving force.

If you stop pedalling there is no driving force, so the resistive forces slow you down. If you need to stop at traffic lights then you apply the brakes to slow you down faster. Pedalling with less force makes the resistive force bigger than the driving force. The bike slows down until the forces are once more in balance, when it continues at a slower but constant speed.

Did You Know?

Lorries and trains use air brakes. Air pressure keeps the brakes off the wheels when the vehicle is moving. When the pressure is released, the brakes are applied. This is a fail-safe system. If a fault causes a leak of air, the brakes are put into operation.

no driving force
*If the driving force is less than the resistive force you **will** slow down*

---

1 The forces acting on a moving car are balanced.

   a Draw a diagram that shows the driving force and resistive forces acting on the car.

   b What happens to the speed of the car when the forces are balanced?

2 Explain why the air resistance acting on a moving cyclist becomes greater as the cyclist travels faster.

3 Explain how the motion of a cyclist is affected:

   a if there is a head wind,

   b if there is a tail wind.

6.06 The Earth's pull

Falling down

Drop a penny and it falls to the ground. Throw a ball in the air and it comes back down. All over the world, things are constantly falling down.

Isaac Newton is reported to have made his discovery about why things fall down after seeing an apple fall from a tree. This may or may not be true, but the answer he came up with is quite simple; things fall down because there is a force pulling them down.

You already know that forces are caused by *something* pushing or pulling *something else*. You also know that you cannot push or pull *something else* unless you touch it or are connected to it in some way. This is why scientists are doubtful when someone claims to be able to bend objects without touching them. What seems strange about the force that pulls things down is that there is no obvious method of contact.

However, the downward force that pulls things towards the centre of the Earth is not the only force that can pull things without any contact. If you have ever played with magnets you know that magnets can pull and push other magnets without touching them.

What causes this downward force? The answer is the Earth itself. It pulls things towards it. So the correct description of the force that makes an apple fall from a tree is 'the Earth pulls the apple'.

The Earth's gravitational force (gravity) pulls the apple towards the centre of the Earth.

Your dog cannot pull you along without a lead connecting you

Did You Know?

Isaac Newton is famous for his theory of gravitation. Few people know that he also invented the 17th century equivalent of the cat flap.

About gravitational forces

Isaac Newton realized that not only does the Earth pull things towards it but that *every object pulls every other object*. The pulling forces between everyday objects are tiny. They are much too small to make them move together. Stars and planets and their moons are very massive objects and they exert pulling forces that are big enough to make things move towards them. These forces are called **gravitational forces**. (Unlike magnetic forces they can only pull, they cannot push).

---

1. Write down *two* examples of forces that can pull or push without touching the object that they are pulling or pushing.

2. The Earth pulls things towards it.
   a Draw diagrams to show the Earth's pull on:
      i   the Moon
      ii you
      iii an apple on a tree.
   b Write a description of each force in **a**.

3. The Moon's gravitational pull is weaker than that of the Earth.

   Imagine that you are on the Moon. Write a description of your Moon walk.

Air can push

6.07

Air resistance

If you drop a ball or a coin from shoulder height, the Earth pulls it down to the ground. The Earth's pull on the ball is an unbalanced force and so the ball speeds up all the time it is in the air. Because it is not falling for very long it does not travel fast. The force of air resistance on the ball is so small that it does not affect the motion at all. Falling with only the Earth pulling you and nothing pushing you back is called **free-fall motion.**

Repeating the experiment with a sheet of paper can lead to very different results. If the paper is scrunched up it falls like the ball. If the sheet of paper is held horizontally and released, it swirls around and takes much longer to reach the ground. Because of its large surface area, air resistance affects the motion of the sheet of paper even at low speeds.

Parachutes

When a sky-diver jumps out of an aircraft the force due to air resistance is small and so his speed increases rapidly. As the sky-diver goes faster the air resistance increases. When the force of the Earth's pull on the sky-diver and the air resistance are balanced he travels at a constant speed, called the terminal velocity. Sky-divers without parachutes can reach vertical speeds of more than 160 kmph (kilometers per hour) (100 mph).

Opening the parachute increases the surface area and this in turn increases the air resistance. With the resistive force now bigger than the driving force, the sky-diver slows down. As the sky-diver's speed becomes less, so does the force of the air resistance. A new terminal velocity is reached when the sky-diver has slowed down to a speed where the resistive force and the driving force are balanced again. The terminal velocity reached with the parachute open is slower than the terminal velocity before the parachute was opened. The sky-diver can land without being injured.

> **Did You Know?**
> The fastest speed recorded by a person in free-fall is 625 m.p.h.

Vertically: air resistance is small. The sky-diver travels very fast.

Vertically: air resistance is bigger so the sky-diver travels more slowly.

---

1. Draw diagrams that show the forces on a parachutist who is

   a speeding up

   b slowing down

   c travelling at terminal velocity.

2. When a space probe is sent to another planet it speeds up as it approaches the planet.

   a What force causes the probe to speed up?

   Probes are often fitted with parachutes to slow them down as they enter a planet's atmosphere.

   b Explain why the space probe needs to be slowed down.

   c Explain why Moon probes are not fitted with parachutes.

3. The graph shows how the vertical speed of a parachutist changes after she leaves an aircraft. Describe what is happening on each of the sections labelled A, B, C and D.

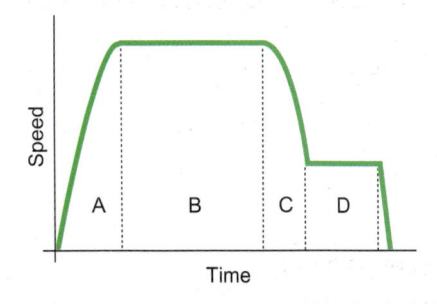

81

Finding out: Falling down

Which falls faster, a light object or a heavy one?

Write down what you think, together with your reasons.

Instructions

1. Hold two masses, a heavy one and a light one, one in each hand. Release them at the same time from the same height and listen for the noises as they reach the ground. Write down what you have found out.

2. Now try with a mass and a scrap of paper. Can you explain the differences in the motion of the mass and the paper?

3. Time how long it takes for a sheet of paper to fall to the ground when it is dropped in three different ways.

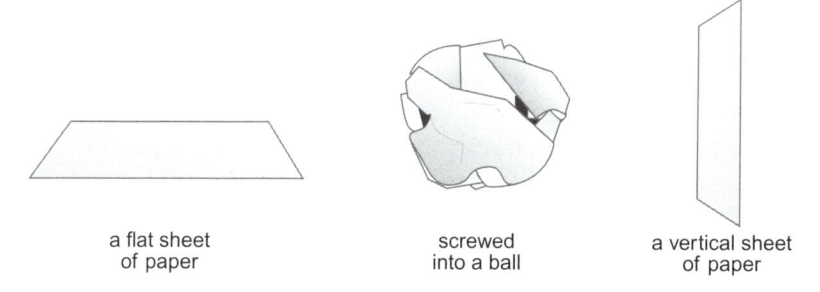

a flat sheet of paper

screwed into a ball

a vertical sheet of paper

   a How will you make sure that the test is fair?

   b You should take several timings for each piece of paper and record your results in a table like this:

Paper	Time for the paper to fall to the ground/ s			Average time for paper to fall/ s $\left(\frac{first + second + third}{3}\right)$
	first reading	second reading	third reading	
Flat sheet				
Ball				
Vertical sheet				

4. a What have you found out? Write a summary of your results.

   b Are all your results reliable, or are there any odd ones?

   c Explain your findings in terms of the force acting on the paper.

Sinking

6.08

If you drop a marble or a coin in some water it sinks. Ships that are made out of iron can float. Whether an object floats or sinks depends on the forces that act on it. People who design ships and submarines have to work out the forces very carefully. They have to be sure that the vessels they design will not sink to the bottom of the sea.

Upward and downward forces

One force that acts on all objects is the downward force of the Earth's pull. This force is also called the object's **weight**. A one kilogram iron mass weighs about 10 N and a brick weighs about 25 N.

The diagram below shows what happens as you lower a brick into a bucket of water.

This submarine needs to be able to sink as well as float

The brick weighs 25 N

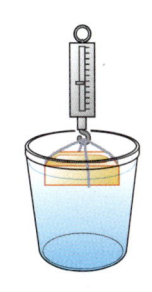

The reading has gone down

The brick now seems to weigh only 15 N

As the brick goes into the water the reading on the forcemeter goes down. It continues to drop until the whole of the brick is under water.

The brick seems to get lighter because the water pushes up on it. The size of the upward push from the water depends on how much of the brick is under the water surface. As the brick enters the water the upward push gets bigger. It reaches a steady size when all the brick is under water.

A brick sinks in water because the downward force is always bigger than the upward force. These two forces are unbalanced. The Earth's downward pull on the brick is always bigger than the upward push from the water, so the brick goes down.

Did You Know?

One of the world's worst shipping disasters occurred in 1912 when the *Titanic* sank on its maiden voyage. The ship was designed to be unsinkable, but an iceberg made holes in five of its sixteen watertight compartments.

---

1 a List five objects that sink when placed in water and five objects that float.
  b What do the objects that sink have in common?
  c What do the objects that float have in common?

2 Use diagrams to explain why a stone seems to become lighter when it is placed under water.

3 The captain of a submarine can make it float or sink. Suggest how a floating submarine can be made to sink.

83

6.09 Floating

When an iron block is placed in water it sinks because the downward pull of the Earth is greater than the upward push of the water. Iron ships float and empty oil drums made from iron can be used to make rafts. Whether an object floats or sinks does not depend only on what material it is made from. The shape and how much air it contains are also important factors.

Forces in balance

If you push a ball or a balloon under water you can feel the water pushing it back up. The further down you push it, the bigger this upward force becomes. Let go and the ball is pushed up to the water surface.

The size of the upward push depends on the volume that is submerged. When all of the ball is under water the force is bigger than when only half of it is under.

The ball floats when there is just enough of it under the water to make the upward and downward forces equal. If it is pushed down the upward force becomes bigger than the weight and so it moves up when it is released.

Floating a ship

A lump of Plasticine sinks in water, but it can be made to float by changing its shape. By making it into a bowl or dish shape it takes up a bigger volume under water, so the upward push from the water is greater than when it is in a lump. The same thing happens with a ship.

Ships contain a lot of air, so the total volume is much greater than the volume of the iron used to make the ship. The ship floats with just enough volume under the water to make the upward and downward forces balance. When the ship takes on cargo and passengers the downward forces increase. This causes the ship to sink lower in the water. With a greater volume of the ship under water there is also a greater upward force. The forces are once more balanced with a greater volume of the ship under water.

This ship weighs thousands of tonnes, but it stays afloat

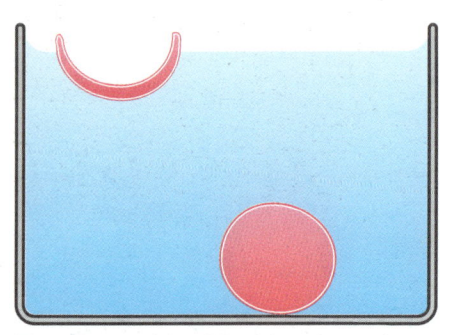

The shape of the Plasticine determines whether it floats or sinks

---

1 A ship floats on water.

　a Draw a diagram of a floating ship. Draw arrows to show the forces and write descriptions of the forces.

　b Explain why the forces on a floating ship are 'balanced'.

2 Ice floats on water. Most of an iceberg is under water. Explain how icebergs can be dangerous to ships.

3 Oil tankers carry thousands of tonnes of oil. Draw diagrams that show an oil tanker floating when it is fully loaded and when it is empty. Explain why the diagrams are different.

Raising a wreck

6.10

There are many wrecked ships on the beds of the world's oceans and seas. Some are of historical importance and others may contain valuable objects or clues as to why the ship sank. Bringing the remains of a wrecked ship to the surface is a very difficult and costly job.

A floating ship can weigh thousands of tonnes, but when it is lying on the seabed it can weigh much more than this because it maybe covered with mud and silt.

Unbalanced forces

For the ship to move upwards towards the surface, there has to be an unbalanced force acting upwards. This force is created by using enormous balloons that are filled with air when they are under water.

First, the balloons are attached to the wreck using cables. Then they are slowly filled with air. This creates an upward force from the water. As more air is pumped into the balloons this upward force gets bigger. As soon as the upward force is bigger than the downward force, (the weight of the ship plus any mud and silt) the ship starts to rise. When raising an 'old' ship great care needs to be taken to stop it from breaking up due to the very large opposing forces acting on it.

The ship starts to rise to the surface, because the forces acting on it are unbalanced. To make it start moving, the upward push from the water has to be greater than the downward forces on it.

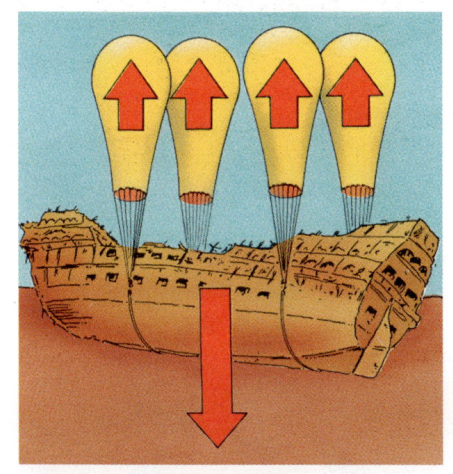

The Mary Rose sank in 1545. It was raised in 1982 using balloons attached to a 'cradle'. Over 13 000 items were recovered from the wreck.

The upward force from the water increases as the balloons fill with air

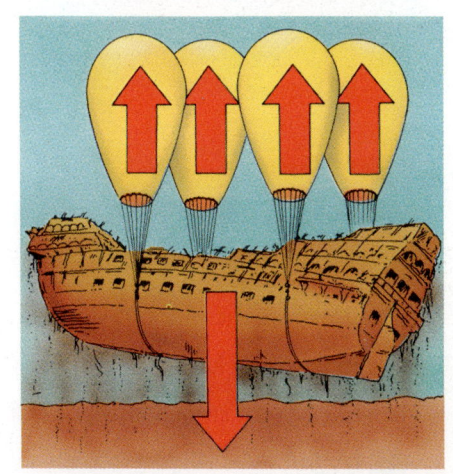

The ship starts to rise when the forces are unbalanced (greater force upwards)

1. Write a statement about the upward and downward forces on the ship when it is:
   a starting to rise from the seabed
   b rising at a constant speed.

2. Explain how the forces that act on a wreck being raised from the seabed are similar to those on a hot-air balloon as it rises from the ground. You should draw a diagram showing the forces on the balloon.

3. One of the downward forces on the ship is the weight of the water above it.
   a Explain how the size of this force changes as the wreck approaches the surface.
   b How does this affect the balance of the forces acting on the ship?
   c How could this affect the motion of the ship as it gets nearer to the surface?

85

6.11 Forces that stretch

Forces and shape
Everything that we do involves forces. Forces are needed to make things move and to stop things from moving. They cause things to speed up or slow down or change direction. Forces also cause a change in shape and size. Sometimes this is a very obvious change, when you stretch a rubber band for example. On other occasions the change is very small and not noticeable. You do not notice the change in shape of a concrete floor when you walk across it.

The sport of Bungee-jumping only started in 1990 (in New Zealand). It uses stretchy ropes.

Elastic or plastic
When you get out of bed in the morning, you expect the mattress to go back to the shape it was before you got on it.

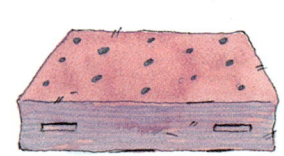

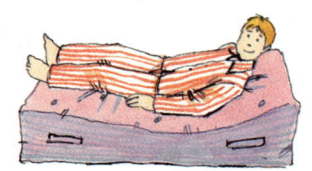

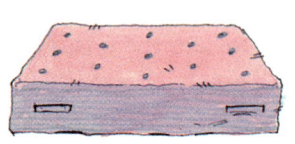

The mattress changes shape when you lie on it and goes back when you get off

When you get dressed you need to stretch your socks to be able to put them on, but you do not expect them to stay stretched. These are examples of things that are **elastic**. Elastic objects change their shape when a force acts on them but they go back to their original shape and size when the force is taken away.

If you take a flat piece of Blu-tack and shape it into a ball, you do not expect it to go back to a flat sheet. Blu-tack, playdough and Plasticine are **plastic** materials. They can be reshaped using forces and they keep their new shape after the force is taken away.

Plasticine is plastic – it keeps its new shape

---

1 Which of these are elastic and which are plastic?

rubber   sock   bed spring   butter

Plasticine   string   rubber band

2 a List five everyday objects that stretch easily.

b For each object in your list, explain why it needs to stretch easily.

3 How could you find out whether nylon fishing line is elastic or plastic? Use diagrams to describe what you would do. Explain how you would reach a conclusion from your results.

Finding out: Springs

Springs are useful because when you stretch them, they pull back. In this experiment you will find out if a spring stretches in a regular way.

Instructions

1. Measure the length of the spring with no force on it. Record this in a table like the one shown below.

2. Carefully place a 100 g mass on the end of the spring, so that the spring does not bounce about. This causes a stretching force of 1 N. Measure and record the new length of the spring.

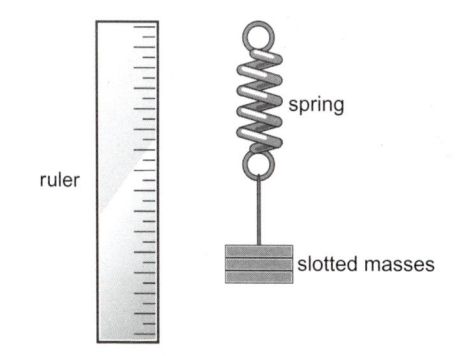

Stretching force/ N	Length of spring/ cm	Length of spring/ cm when force is removed	Does the spring return to its original length when the force is removed?
0			

3. Remove the load and check the length of the spring. Record this in your table.

4. Repeat steps 2 and 3, increasing the force by 1 N each time. Your teacher will tell you the greatest force that it is safe to apply. **DO NOT EXCEED THIS.** Remember to remove the force and check the length of the spring after each 1 N increase.

5. Use your results to draw a line graph of *length of spring* against *stretching force*. See if you can work out suitable scales to use.

6. Describe the pattern that the graph shows.

WARNING

Always wear eye protection when working with springs.

87

6.12 Using springs

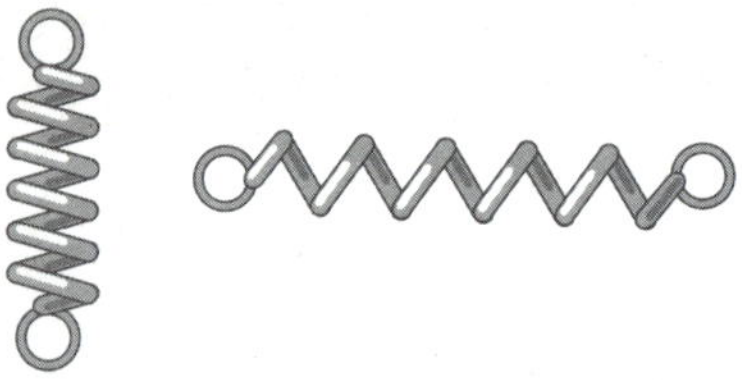

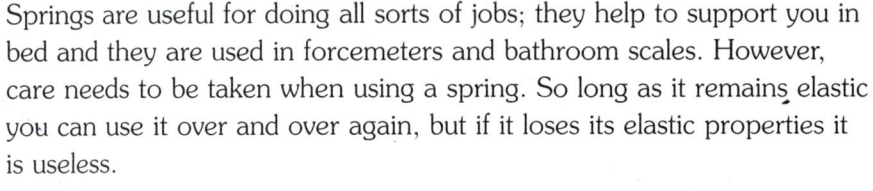

Springs are useful for doing all sorts of jobs; they help to support you in bed and they are used in forcemeters and bathroom scales. However, care needs to be taken when using a spring. So long as it remains elastic you can use it over and over again, but if it loses its elastic properties it is useless.

Each spring is elastic for a certain range of force, but if it is stretched beyond this range it becomes permanently extended and it will not go back. Manufacturers who use springs in things such as children's toys need to be sure that they cannot be overstretched.

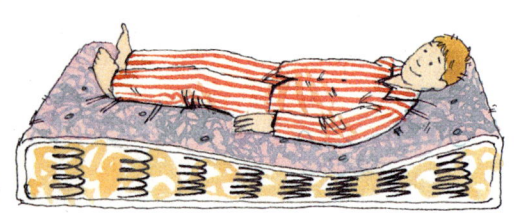

this spring is still elastic

but this spring is plastic

Lying in bed

When you are lying in bed you are not only resting, you are also at rest in the sense that you are not moving. The forces on you are balanced. This means that the mattress has to push up on you with a force that is equal in size to your weight, the downward pull of the Earth on you. Bed springs are compression springs; if you push down on a bed spring it gets smaller (compresses) and pushes back up on you. This is how the mattress supports you when you are in bed. As you rest your weight on a bed, the springs compress until they push up on you with a force equal in size to the downward pull of the Earth on you (your weight).

The springs compress to support your weight

Weighing a baby

Young babies need to be weighed frequently to check that they are gaining weight. The forcemeter used to weigh a baby uses a spring that gets longer when a force pulls it. If you pull on a spring it pulls back with an equal-size force. Suspending the baby from the spring causes the spring to stretch until the forces on the baby are balanced. The spring stops stretching when the upward pull of the spring is equal in size to the downward pull of the Earth (the baby's weight).

The heavier the baby, the more the spring stretches

---

1 a What happens to a spring when it is overstretched?

  b The springs in cycle brakes pull the brake blocks away from the wheels when the cyclist lets go of the brake lever.

  Why is it important that the springs are not overstretched?

  c What could happen if the springs stopped being elastic?

2 a Sketch a line graph that shows how the length of a spring changes when the pulling force is increased. Label the line '1'.

  b A second spring is harder to stretch. Add another line to your graph that shows how the length of this spring changes for the same range of pulling forces. Label this line '2'.

3 How could you find out how much force can be applied to a spring before it loses its elastic property? Use a diagram to show how you would test the spring and explain how you would reach a conclusion.

The idea of reproduction

CHAPTER 7

7.01 SEX IN PLANTS AND ANIMALS

Reproduction is the most important feature of living things. From the biological point of view this is the only reason for living. There are two main ways to do this.

Asexual reproduction

In this method of reproducing an exact copy is made. Cells contain a complete blueprint for the organism. The idea is to take one cell and let it grow into an adult. This is **asexual** (not using sex) **reproduction**.

Many protists (single - celled organisms, such as an *Amoeba*) use asexual reproduction. The cells simply divide and separate. Plants often use this method too. Many plants produce offspring from roots, bulbs, or runners or even leaf bits dropping off! Potatoes are produced asexually and can grow into new plants. Onions are bulbs which will sprout if you leave them. In this way rapid copying of a successful blueprint takes place.
(Cloning also works this way.)

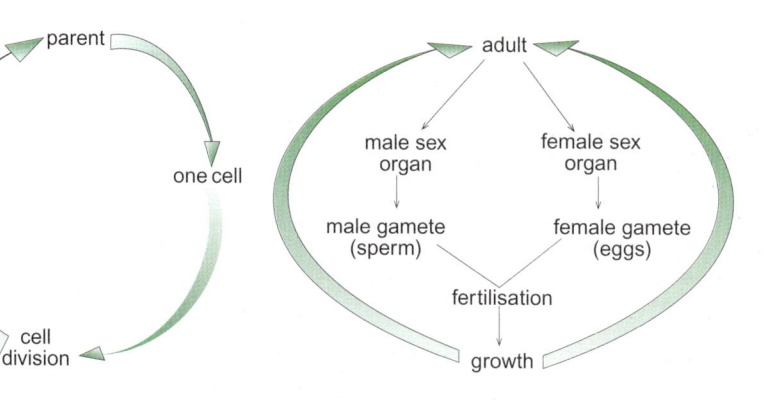

The turtle lives between plated decks

Which practically conceal its sex

I think it clever of the turtle

In such a fix to be so fertile

— Ogden Nash

The asexual ... ... and sexual reproduction cycles

Sexual reproduction

The second way of reproducing is by **sexual reproduction**. There are special male and female cells **(gametes)**. They each provide half the blueprint needed for the new organism. The male sex cell joins with the female one. This is **fertilization**. After fertilization the new cell grows into an adult. For most organisms this approach means there are two parents. This method allows two old blueprints to make a brand new one. Most organisms use this method some of the time.

Frogs mating - sexual reproduction has to get male gametes to female gametes

---

1. What is reproduction?
2. Explain at least one advantage of asexual reproduction.
3. In your own words describe how asexual reproduction happens.
4. What is the advantage of sexual reproduction?
5. In your own words describe how sexual reproduction happens.

7.02

Sexy flowers

Flowering plants reproduce sexually. They are seed plants. They make seeds when they reproduce. The main structure used is the flower.

Some flowers have both male and female organs. Other plants have separate male and female flowers. Holly trees are either male or female and so only the female tree has berries. The willow also has trees with separate sexes. The hazel, however, has separate male and female flowers on the same tree.

Whatever types of flowers plants have, in most cases they avoid self-fertilization. The male organs ripen before, or after, the female ones. This way only male cells from another plant can get to the female cells. So whatever type of flowers a plant has, a good mix of blueprints is made at fertilization.

Flowers have evolved from leaves. In simpler plants there are spore making organs on the backs of leaves. You can see this if you look at ferns. Over millions of years, leaves like these evolved into the special parts of the flower. The first flowers appeared in Cretaceous times. Flowering plants are so successful they now live everywhere.

The drawing below shows the structure of the simple flower of the buttercup cut in half. This is one of the earliest sorts of flowers to develop and is fairly simple in shape.

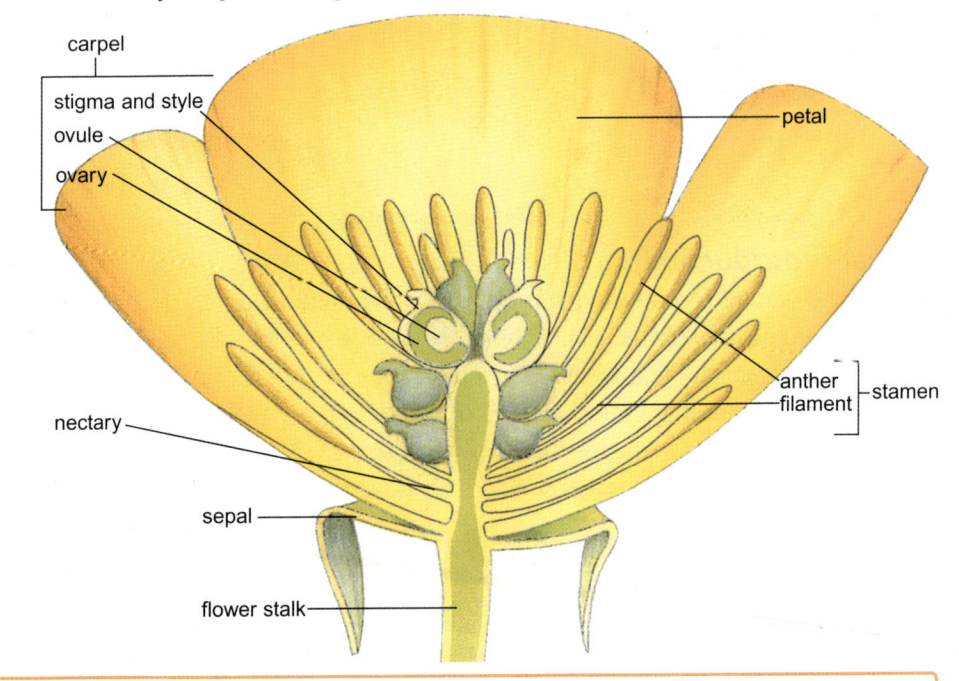

Flowers evolved from leaves, and the first ones looked a bit like these magnolia flowers

The male and female flowers of hazel

A complex flower – each tiny section is a whole flower

What Do You Think?

Why does having seeds make plants successful?

1. Which are the male parts of the flower?
2. Which parts of the flower are female?
3. How do plants avoid self-fertilization?
4. What are the sepals for?

Finding out: Flower structure

Observing and recording flower structure

Flowers are beautifully adapted for their job. It is worth taking a close look at the detailed structure of some to see how they work. The techniques for study are fairly straightforward. You will need to keep a record of what you find. This means learning to draw accurately what you see.

Biological drawings are designed for clarity and accuracy. They are not intended as artistic representations. This means we tend to use outlines and no shading. This allows a careful and accurate record to be kept, although it may lose some of the sense of beauty you get from an artist's picture or the real thing.

WARNING

Scalpels are very sharp and can cut you

A daffodil flower cut in half

Draw what you see

Instructions

1. Take a regular shaped flower like a buttercup. Remove two adjacent petals by pulling near the base with tweezers.
2. Now use a scalpel to cut vertically through the central part of the flower and stem. This should leave you with a flower cut in half with three petals still attached behind it.
3. Use a hand lens to look at the cut central sections.
4. Draw what you see. Make the drawing at least half a page in size.
5. Now take a bilaterally (two-sided) symmetrical flower like a white dead nettle. Cut it vertically along the line of symmetry. Again draw what you see.
6. Both these flowers use insect pollination.
    a. In what way are their structures helpful in this?
    b. Would you expect different types of insect to pollinate them?
    c. What sorts of insects would you expect to find doing this job?
    d. What 'structural' evidence do you have to support these ideas?

7.03 The go-betweens

The first step in flower reproduction is to get the male and female cells together. The male sex cells are carried in the **pollen** grains so plants need to move the pollen to the female part of another flower. They need a go-between. One go-between is the wind. With luck the pollen is blown by the wind and lands on another flower. Another go-between is insects which are attracted to the flower. Pollen sticks to them and they then carry it to another flower.

Wind pollination

This is a chancy business! Some plants make very light pollen. This will blow around easily. If they are relying on the wind, they will need to make lots of pollen because most of it will go to waste. On wind-pollinated plants, the male parts hang out of the flower. The wind shakes them to release the pollen. The female parts need long feathery **stigmas** to catch the pollen. The petals are usually not very important.

Insect pollination

This is a safer way of getting pollen to another flower. The plant makes nectar which attracts insects who use it as fuel. They make the nectar hard to get at so that the insect has to brush against the **anthers**. On insect-pollinated flowers the anthers are short and strong so they do not break. The pollen grains need to be sticky or ridged so they stick to the insect. This means they are usually bigger than wind-pollinated grains. The female parts need to be sticky to pull the pollen off the insect. The flower attracts the insect by smell and by the bright colour of the petals.

Grass produces huge amounts of pollen that can cause hayfever

Small flowers are arranged in large heads that can easily be seen by insects

Did You Know?

Bats can pollinate flowers.

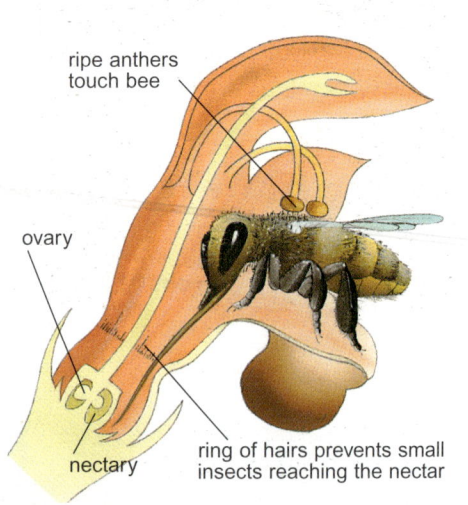

When the insect moves on to another plant it touches a ripe stigma and pollen is transferred

(labels: ripe anthers touch bee; ovary; nectary; ring of hairs prevents small insects reaching the nectar)

1. Using the information above, copy and fill in the table shown below. In each column explain how the part named is adapted to each sort of pollination.

	Wind-pollinated	Insect-pollinated
Petals		
Pollen		
Male parts		
Female parts		

2. Look at the picture of an insect pollinating a flower. In your own words explain how the flower is adapted for pollination.

3. What do insects gain during the process of pollination?

Plants really do mate

7.04

Once the pollen grain reaches the stigma of another plant the most risky part of the male cell's journey has been done. The male cells inside the pollen grain need to get inside the ovary. To do this a tube grows down from the grain. This tube grows down the style and through the **ovary** wall using food from the cells there. The tube grows until it is near the **micropyle**. This is a very small pore in the wall surrounding the **ovule**. The tube grows towards a chemical, called a hormone, produced by the ovule.

After this the male sex cells move down the tube and into the ovule. One of the male sex cells fuses with the waiting egg and fertilizes it.

Seed formation

The details of what happens next vary from one plant species to another. Usually, the following things happen. The fertilized egg divides inside the ovule to form an embryo. It uses food from the old ovule. The walls of the ovule toughen up and the whole thing is now called a seed.

The walls of the ovary become the fruit. In biology fruits include tomatoes, marrows, pods (e.g. peas) and conker shells as well as the obvious ones. You can always tell a fruit because it has seeds (or pips) inside it.

The flowers wither away, often becoming just a small hook or shrivelled end on the fruit. The seeds usually enter a period of dormancy now until they are shed and land in the right place to germinate.

There are many ways for fruit to shed seeds. Some plants rely on animals to eat the fruit and pass the seeds out with their waste. Some fruit blow in the wind and shake the seeds out. Others shoot the seeds out. Each fruit is adapted to a particular way of spreading the seeds out.

Dandelion, broom, and plum fruits

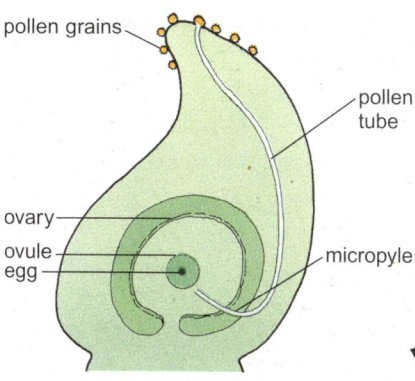

The pollen tube grows using food from the female parts of the flower

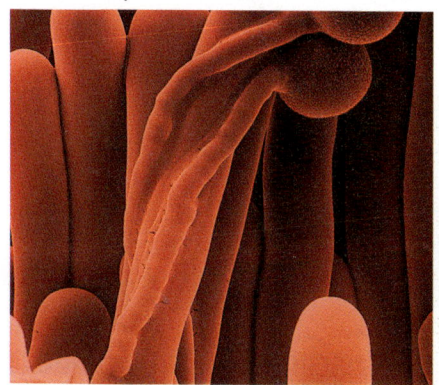

Many pollen grains start growing in this poppy flower. Only one will fertilize the egg

The embryo has just started to grow from the seed. It puts out a root and a shoot

1 Why do you think only one pollen tube gets to the micropyle?

2 What might stop pollen tubes growing from pollen grains from other species?

3 Look at the photos of fruit and seeds above. Explain how each is adapted to disperse or spread the seeds.

Finding out: Pollen and pollen tubes

It is interesting to see close up the details of the growth of the pollen tube. To be able to see this clearly you will need a reasonably large flower, like a daffodil or a tulip.

> **WARNING**
>
> Methylene blue stains

Instructions: pollen grains

1. Remove a stamen and place it on a slide. Crush the tip with your tweezers.
2. Put a drop of water on the tip and gently place a cover slip on top.
3. View the slide under the microscope. Remember to start with the lowest power lens and the tube racked down.
4. You should be able to see the pollen grains. What shape are they? How big are they?

Instructions: pollen tubes

1. Get another stamen and two cavity slides.
2. Shake some pollen into the cavity of each slide.
3. Put two drops of water in the cavity of one slide and two drops of weak sugar solution in the cavity of the other.
4. Put a cover slip over each cavity and label the slides clearly. Leave the slides for several hours.
5. Look at the slides under the low power of the microscope only.
6. You should be able to see pollen tubes growing.
7. On which slide did they grow best? What would you expect to find in the style of the female parts of the plant?

Instructions: style and stigma

1. Remove the stigma and style of the flower.
2. Put them on a slide and cover them with methylene blue. Leave them for five minutes.
3. Wash the stigmas and styles in a beaker of clean water by gently dipping them in.
4. Put them onto a clean slide in a drop of water and put a cover slip on top.
5. Look at the style and stigma under the low power of the microscope.
6. Which parts have stained blue?
7. Can you see pollen tubes? Are all the pollen grains the same? If there are different ones, have any that are not from your flowers grown tubes?

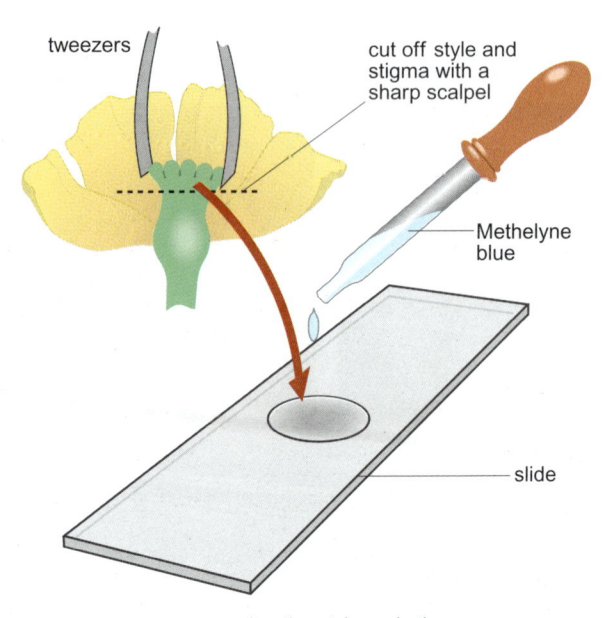

removing the style and stigma

The human life cycle

7.05

Like all animals, people have a life cycle. We are either male or female and reproduce sexually. Each person produces sex cells (**gametes**) which can fuse in a process called **fertilization**. The new cell formed is a **zygote**. It grows inside the mother into a new individual.

> **How Good is Your Memory?**
>
> Can you remember being a zygote? How far back can you go?

Puberty or adolescence

The youngster has to mature enough before he or she can reproduce. When old enough, the body changes so that reproduction can occur. It makes sex cells and in girls the womb gets ready for a baby. These changes happen during **puberty** or **adolescence.** Adolescence also involves a change of feelings towards other people. People become sexually attracted. This can sometimes be very hard to cope with. Adolescence is the time when someone is changing from being a child to an adult. These changes evolved originally to help the species to survive. Humans belong to the order of primates and like most other primates, males defend territory and females need protection when pregnant.

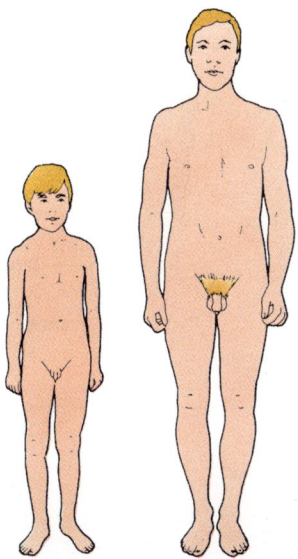

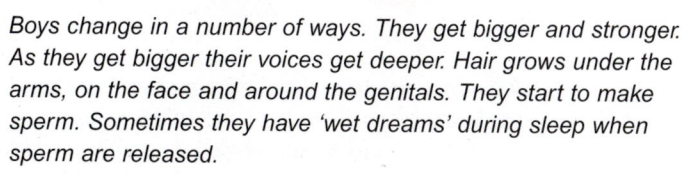

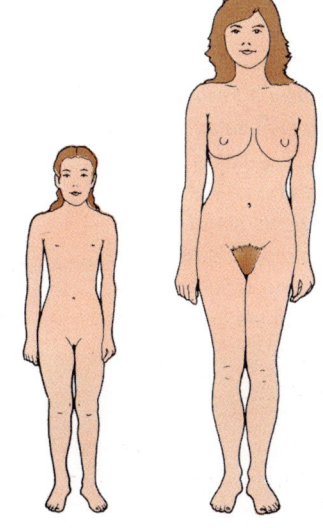

Boys change in a number of ways. They get bigger and stronger. As they get bigger their voices get deeper. Hair grows under the arms, on the face and around the genitals. They start to make sperm. Sometimes they have 'wet dreams' during sleep when sperm are released.

Girls change too. They develop breasts and broader hips. They also grow hair under their arms and around the genitals. Eggs start to develop and the womb begins the monthly cycle that prepares for a baby. At the end of each cycle the womb loses its lining causing bleeding (the 'period').

1 Make a table in your book as shown. Fill in the changes that occur in boys and girls. The first one has been done for you.

Changes in girls	Changes in boys
Eggs develop	Sperm are made

2 Draw a picture of the life cycle of human beings.

3 What is adolescence?

95

7.06 Human reproduction ♂ (male)

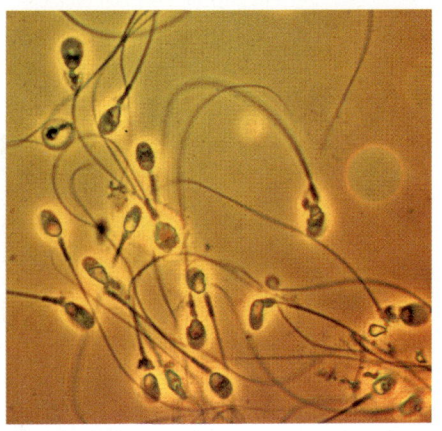

Human sexual systems are fairly typical of mammals. A mature man makes **sperm** all the time. They are made in his **testicles** (testes). The sperm are tiny cells with a half set of instructions for making a new person. The instructions are in the head of the cell. Each cell also has a long tail which helps it move. Because they are so small, sperm live in a liquid food supply. The liquid (semen) contains sugar. This gives the cells the energy they need.

Sperm cells

The testes and other glands make semen. The movement of sperm out of the body (an ejaculation) is muscular. The muscles in the tubes squeeze the sperm and semen out together. This is a bit like squeezing toothpaste out of the tube.

The **penis** has special tissue inside it. When the head of the penis is stimulated blood is pumped into this tissue. The blood goes in faster than it comes out and so the tissue swells. This makes the penis stand up (an erection). This is a simple built in response and happens even in young children. In mature men continued stimulation leads to an ejaculation.

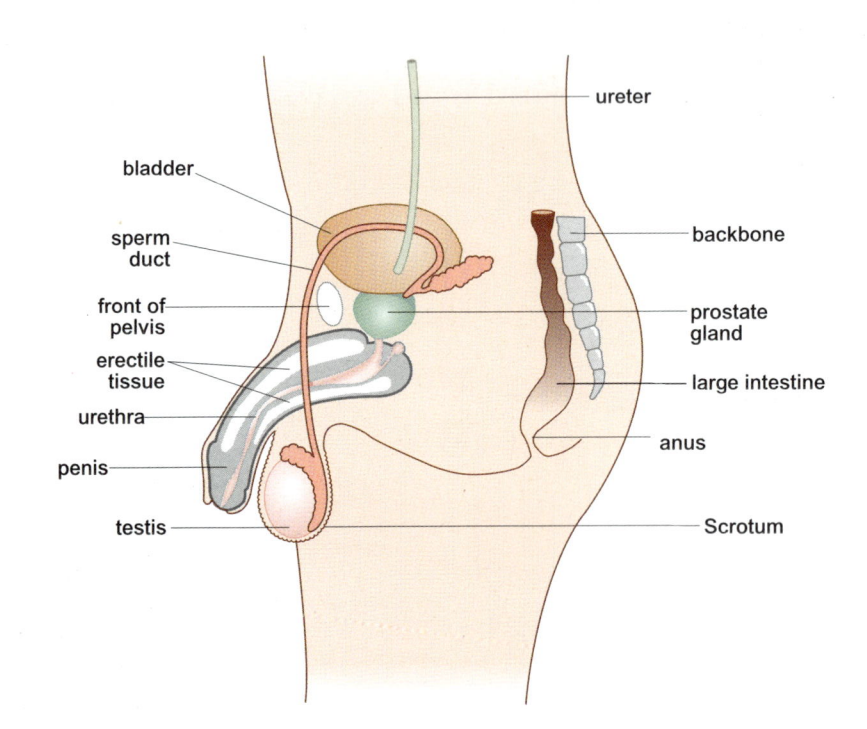

Labels: ureter, bladder, sperm duct, front of pelvis, erectile tissue, urethra, penis, testis, backbone, prostate gland, large intestine, anus, Scrotum

When they are born, boys have a sheath of skin (the foreskin) covering the head of the penis. This helps protect it. Sometimes the foreskin is removed for medical reasons or because of religious customs. It makes no difference to how the penis works later in life.

What Do You Think?

Sperm count in Europe is declining. What could be the cause?

1. What is semen?
2. Describe how an erection and ejaculation happen.
3. Why do sperm need a food supply outside them?
4. What does the foreskin do?

Human reproduction ♀ (female)

7.07

Girls are born with all the **eggs** they will ever have. These eggs live in the **ovaries**. When a woman is mature the eggs ripen. One egg ripens every month. This means that each ovary ripens an egg once every two months. The egg fills up with food until it is about the size of a printed full stop. It grows in a 'bubble' of cells called a follicle. The cells of the follicle transfer food into the egg. The follicle gets bigger as well and eventually bursts.

At this point the egg passes into the oviduct or fallopian tube. This tube has a lining of cells with small hairs. The hairs beat and help waft the egg along the tube to the womb. If the egg is not fertilized, it passes out of the womb down the vagina. If it is fertilized, it sticks to the womb lining and starts to grow into a baby.

The breasts are also part of the reproductive system. When a woman is pregnant her breasts grow. This is due to the development of special cells that will make milk for the baby.

> **What Do You Think?**
>
> More girls than boys survive to adulthood. Why?

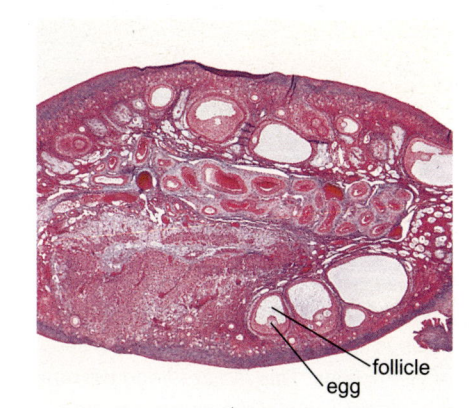

A cross section of an ovary. It shows several follicles at different stages.

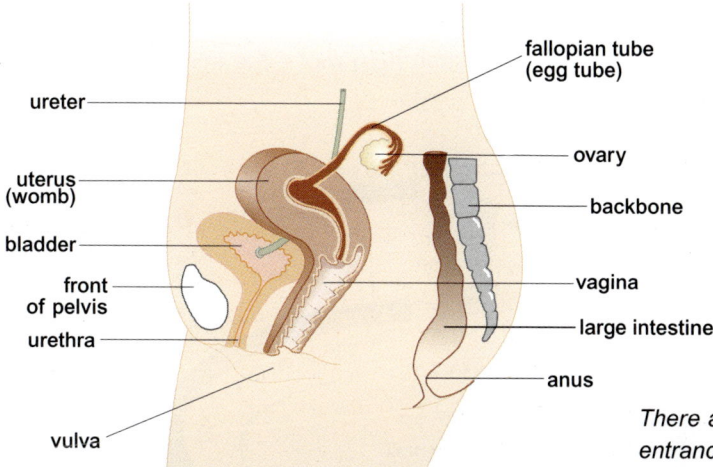

*There are folds of skin (labia) over the entrance to the **vagina**. This protects the entrances to the vagina and urethra. Inside these folds is a small area called the clitoris. This is very sensitive to touch. During intercourse stimulation of the clitoris causes a reflex to occur which helps lubricate the vagina.*

1. Describe how an egg ripens.
2. How is the egg moved to the womb?
3. What do the labia do?
4. Why do the breasts grow in pregnancy?

7.08 Menstrual cycle/fertilization

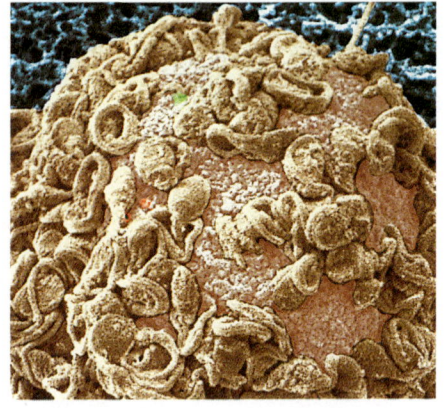

The female system is a bit more complex than the male. This is because it has to be able to support the development of a baby. An egg ripens every month and the womb has to be ready for a fertilized egg. The womb lining thickens gradually during the first half of the monthly cycle. It is rich with blood to bring food to the baby. The womb lining gets to its thickest at the same time as the egg leaves the fallopian tube.

Unfertilized eggs pass out of the body and the lining of the womb breaks down. The body does not need a thick lining to the womb until the next egg ripens in a month's time. So the thickened part of the womb lining breaks down. This loss of the lining is the 'period'. During her period the woman loses blood. It is important to eat a healthy diet to replace the chemicals lost in the blood, especially iron. This monthly change in the lining is the menstrual cycle. Chemicals called hormones control the cycle.

For the egg to be fertilized the sperm have to meet it. The sperm enter the woman during intercourse. The penis fits into the vagina helped by lubrication from secretions made there. The close contact stimulates an ejaculation. Semen and sperm are pushed into the neck of the womb. Muscular movements in the womb help move the sperm into the fallopian tube. Here the sperm meet the egg.

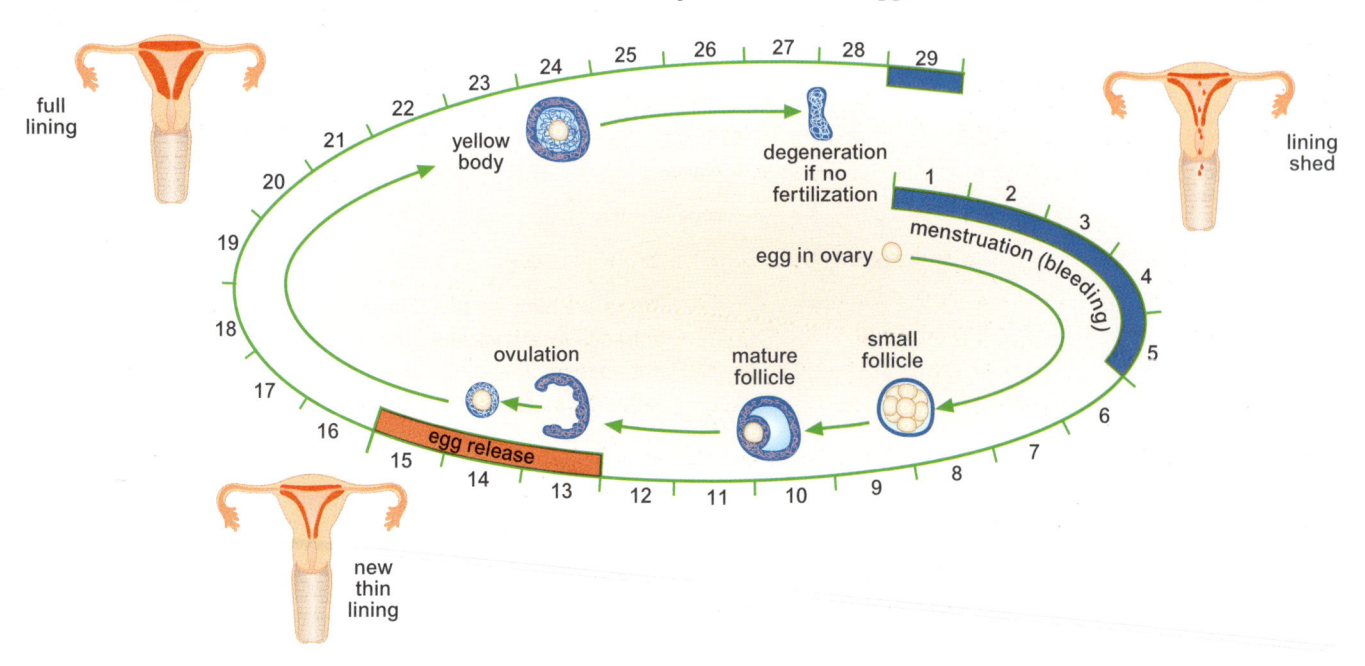

Fertilization: Only one sperm cell reaches and penetrates the egg. Immediately this has happened, the egg changes chemically to stop other sperm getting in. The male nucleus fuses with the female nucleus. This forms a cell with a full set of instructions. This fertilized egg will now stick to the lining of the womb and start to develop into a baby.

Timings within the menstrual cycle and the length of the menstrual cycle vary from person to person

1. Draw a diagram of the menstrual cycle and describe what happens.
2. Why is it important for a woman to eat extra foods containing iron during her period?
3. Why is it important to stop more than one sperm entering an egg?

98

The baby grows

7.09

What Do You Think?

Is having babies more efficient than laying eggs?

The fertilized egg contains the blueprint for a new individual. Yet it is only one cell. You contain millions of cells, many of which are specialized. How do all these cells develop from just one? The story of the growth of a fertilized egg in mammals is one of the wonders of nature.

The fertilized egg (**zygote**) divides several times to form a ball of cells (**blastula**). It is this that sticks to the side of the womb. Once it is attached, the womb lining grows out round it. Some of the blastula cells then grow connections to the lining. This structure becomes the placenta. The placenta is a mixture of tissues from the mother and the baby. This is vital for the baby's survival. It allows the mother and baby to exchange food and wastes without the mother's and baby's blood actually mixing.

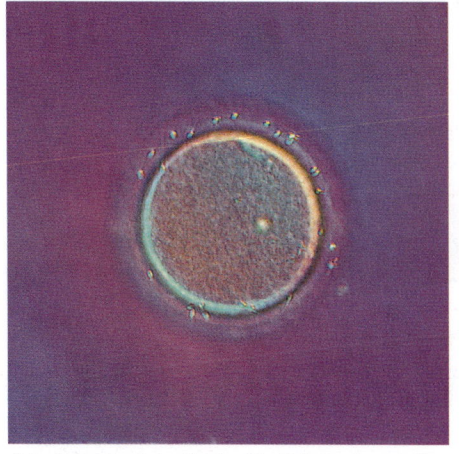

It is the blastula that will stick to the wall of the womb

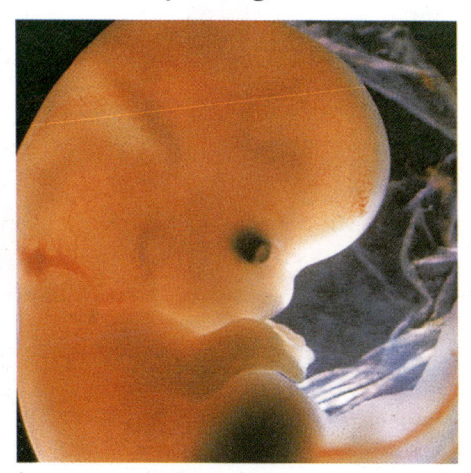

A seven week-old embryo

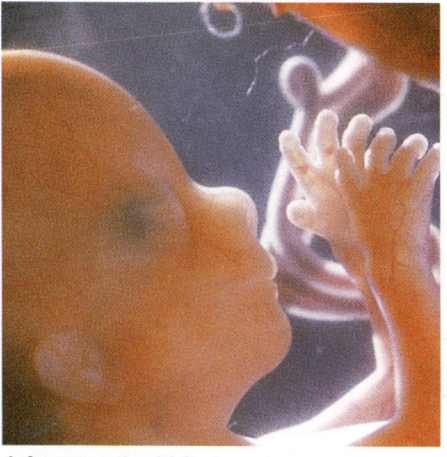

A four month-old foetus

Another part of the blastula grows to become the **embryo**. How do cells 'know' whether to become placenta or embryo? We believe this is controlled by chemicals. We think that they give information to the cells as to where they are. As a result, cells 'read' different parts of the blueprint. This lets them grow into the specialized cells that the body needs.

The embryo is called a **foetus** once it looks essentially human (at about three months). After this it grows bigger until birth. The placenta transfers food from the mother's blood to the baby. Wastes from the baby pass back to the mother for her to remove. The mother also passes important defences against disease, in the form of **antibodies**, to the baby. After nine months the baby is ready to be born.

1. Explain how the placenta forms.
2. What is the main role of the placenta?
3. How do cells 'know' how to develop?
4. Why do you think the foetus in the picture is surrounded by liquid?

CHAPTER 8

8.01 METALS

What is a metal?

Some of the properties of metals are listed below.

- All metals, apart from mercury, are solids at room temperature.
- Most metals are shiny although lead is dull.
- Metals are usually silvery or brownish in colour.
- Some metals are attracted to a magnet or can be made into magnets. Iron is magnetic.
- Metals are good conductors of heat and electricity.

Did You Know?

Most metals are found in the ground. In the past thirty years scientists have made some metals that do not occur naturally. One of these metals is called Californium and another is called Americum. I am sure you can guess where they were made.

copper (and its ore)   *mercury*   *magnetite (iron ore)*

1 Copy and finish this table, giving examples for each column:

Silver-coloured metals	Browny-coloured metals

2 The table gives the densities of five metals. Some of which are shown in the photographs above.

Metal	Copper	Iron	Gold	Mercury	Lead
Density g/cm³	9	8	20	14	11

The density of water is 1 g/cm³.

a What happens when each of these metals is dropped into water?

b Arrange these five metals in order of their densities. Start with the metal with the lowest density and finish with the metal with the greatest density.

c A small block of gold measures 10 cm × 5 cm × 1 cm. How much does this block weigh?

3 The picture shows a saucepan with a metal handle on a cooker hob. What happens to the handle? Why does this happen?

— metal handle
— saucepan
— gas hob

4 Write a paragraph summarizing the properties that metals usually have. We have mentioned some here but you may be able to think of others.

Finding out: Metals

Testing electrical conductivity

In this experiment you are going to test different substances to see if they conduct electricity.

Instructions

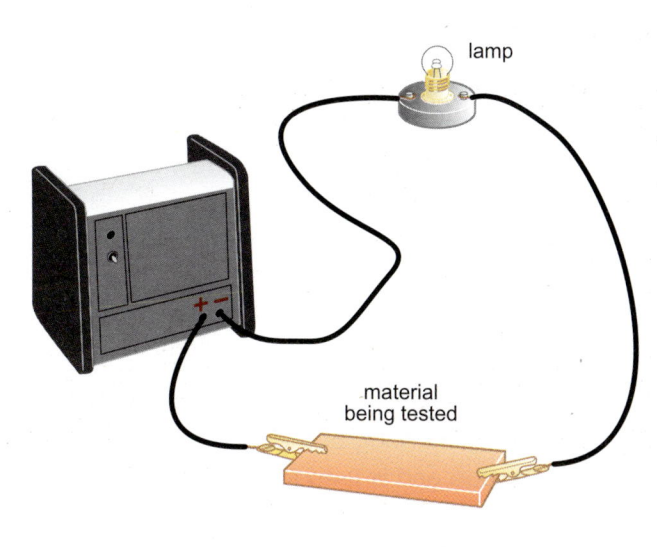

1. Set up the apparatus in the diagram above.
2. Test each of the samples to see if the lamp lights. If the bulb lights the sample conducts electricity.
3. Record your results in a table. If you need help with the table ask your teacher.
4. a Make a list of substances which conduct electricity and substances which do not.
   b Metals conduct electricity and non metals do not. Is this always true?

Reaction of magnesium with dilute acid

Many metals react with dilute hydrochloric acid to produce hydrogen gas. You are going to react magnesium with dilute hydrochloric acid.

Instructions

1. Put 4 cm depth of dilute hydrochloric acid into a test tube. Stand the test tube in a test tube rack.
2. Drop a piece of magnesium ribbon into the acid.
3. Observe all the changes taking place.
4. Hold a lighted splint near the mouth of the tube.
5. Write down all your observations and any conclusions you can make.

WARNING
You must wear goggles when using hydrochloric acid.

8.02 Reactions of metals

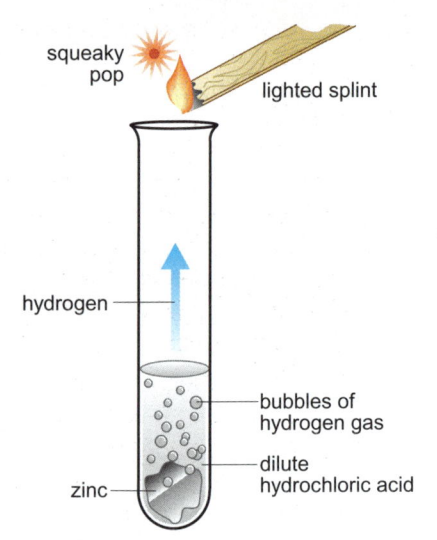

Reactions of metals with air and oxygen
Some metals burn in air or oxygen to form **oxides.** For example you will have seen a piece of magnesium burn with a bright white flame to produce magnesium oxide.

We can summarize this reaction by writing a **word equation:**

magnesium + oxygen → magnesium oxide

The substances on the left hand side of the arrow (magnesium and oxygen) are the starting materials and the substance on the right hand side is the substance produced (magnesium oxide).

Reaction of metals with acid
You have probably tried the reaction of magnesium ribbon with dilute hydrochloric acid. The diagram on the left shows zinc reacting with dilute hydrochloric acid. The fizzing or **effervescence** you can see is caused by bubbles of colourless hydrogen gas being produced. When a metal reacts with a dilute acid it usually produces hydrogen gas.

If a lighted splint is put near the mouth of the test tube, a small explosion may be heard. This is caused by the burning of the hydrogen gas in air. It is sometimes called a squeaky pop and is used to show that hydrogen is present.

Reactions of metals with air and acids
We expect that metals will burn in oxygen to form oxides and will react with dilute acids to produce hydrogen. If a substance does both of these things it is metal. But there are, however, many exceptions – metals that do not burn and do not react with dilute acids.

Zinc reacting with dilute hydrochloric acid

---

1 The picture shows a piece of copper foil before and after heating in air.

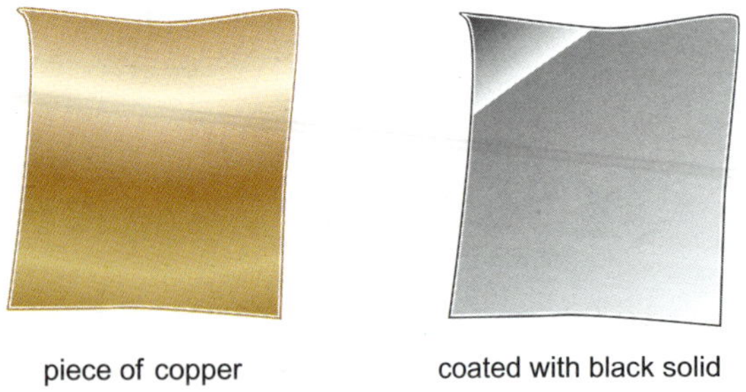

Copper foil before and after heating in air

   a What difference can you see between the two pieces of copper foil?

   b Rosie suggested that the black coating came from soot in the Bunsen burner flame. Josie said it did not but came from oxygen in the air joining with the copper. Who do you think was right? What could you do to prove it?

2 Iron filings burn in air. Write a word equation for the reaction when iron burns.

3 The reaction of magnesium with dilute hydrochloric acid is summarized by this word equation:

magnesium + hydrochloric acid
→ magnesium chloride + hydrogen

Write the word equation for the reaction of zinc with dilute hydrochloric acid.

Metals and non-metals

8.03

Properties of metals

You probably have a good idea of the properties of metals. The table gives the typical physical properties of metals.

Property	What we expect of a typical metal
state	solid
appearance	shiny – silvery or brownish colour
density	high
conductivity	good conductor of both heat and electricity
other properties	can be beaten into a thin sheet – it is said to be **malleable**
	can be drawn into a fine wire – it is said to be **ductile**

Metals often react with dilute acids to form hydrogen gas.

Metals often burn in air or oxygen to form oxides.

Testing the pH values of oxides

The diagram on the right below shows how magnesium can be burned in oxygen to form magnesium oxide. If the oxide formed is tested with universal indicator a pH value of 13 will be noted. This corresponds to forming a strong alkali. In a similar experiment with iron, a pH value of 7 is obtained.

This should be compared with the results if a non-metal such as sulphur is used. The sulphur oxide formed has a pH value of about 2.

Metals burn in oxygen to form alkaline or neutral oxides. Non-metals burn in oxygen to form acidic oxides.

Burning a substance in oxygen and testing the pH value of the residue is the most reliable method of identifying a substance as a metal.

> **Did You Know?**
>
> Appearance is a very unreliable way of deciding whether a substance is a metal or not. Silicon is not a metal but it is a shiny, silvery solid which looks like a metal. Thin wafers of this material are used to make microchips.
>
> Gold can be beaten into such a thin sheet that light can pass through it. This thin gold sheet, called gold leaf, is used for decorating china with gold.

A piece of silicon wafer

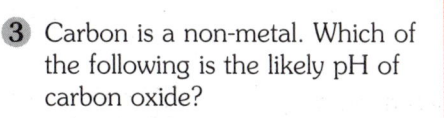

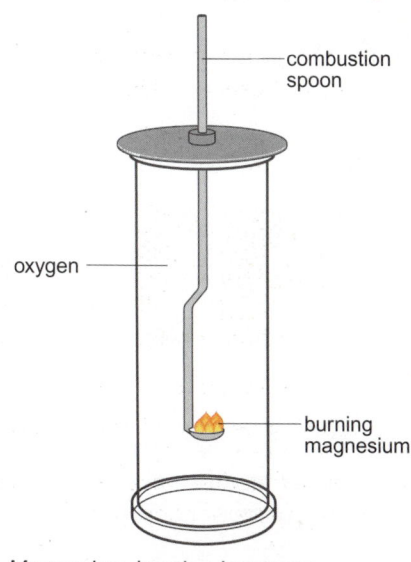

Magnesium burning in oxygen

1. What is the meaning of the word property?
2. Into what two groups do we divide properties?
3. Carbon is a non-metal. Which of the following is the likely pH of carbon oxide?

   5   7   9   13

103

8.04 Metals and alloys

There are about 80 known pure metals.

Pure metals have a wide range of uses. For example, pure copper is used for wiring in your home because it is a good conductor of electricity.

Alloys

Alloys are mixtures of metals or mixtures of metals with other substances such as carbon. They are made because they have more useful properties than pure metals.

For example, ancient peoples found that if they mixed copper and tin together they made an alloy called bronze which was harder than pure copper or pure tin. They used it because it was better for making tools.

The Boeing 747 can fly with up to 500 passengers halfway round the world. To reduce fuel costs it has to weigh as little as possible but the structure must be very strong. Pure aluminium has a low density but is not very strong. The aeroplane is made largely of an aluminium alloy such as magnalium or duralumin which is stronger.

Brass is an important alloy of copper and zinc. It consists of copper with between 18% and 30% zinc. Brass is harder than copper or zinc.

Solder is used to join metals together. For example, two pieces of tin plate can be soldered together. Solder is made of a mixture of tin and lead.

The table gives the melting points of tin, lead and solder. The melting point of solder is much lower than that of tin and lead.

Metal	Melting point/ °C
tin	232
lead	327
solder	about 90

> **Did You Know?**
>
> Gold jewellery can be bought with different qualities of gold. Nine carat gold is cheaper than eighteen carat gold. Both are alloys. Nine carat gold contains less gold and more copper. It is harder than 18 carat gold. 24-carat gold is pure gold.

The Boeing 747 aeroplane is light but strong

---

1. Magnalium is made of 70% aluminium and 30% of another low-density metal. Which metal do you think this is?

2. How does the colour of brass compare with the colour of copper and zinc? Can you think of any uses of brass?

3. Why is the low melting point of solder an advantage when soldering?

4. Can you list some other alloys and their uses?

Corrosion of metals

8.05

The photo on the right shows a steel ship which has been left to rust. Rusting is the name we give to the process where the atmosphere rots away the steel. Some other metals are affected by air in a similar way. The reaction of the metal with air is called **corrosion**. Rusting is an example of corrosion.

What makes steel rust?

The diagram below shows an experiment to find out what causes the rusting of steel. Four test tubes are set up as shown.

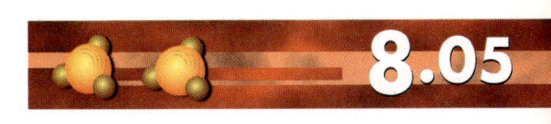

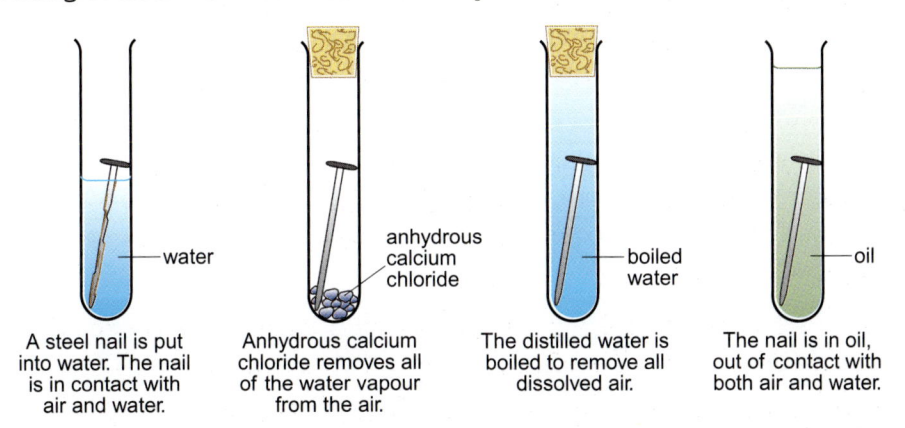

- Tube 1: water — A steel nail is put into water. The nail is in contact with air and water.
- Tube 2: anhydrous calcium chloride — Anhydrous calcium chloride removes all of the water vapour from the air.
- Tube 3: boiled water — The distilled water is boiled to remove all dissolved air.
- Tube 4: oil — The nail is in oil, out of contact with both air and water.

Test tube	What is seen?
1	rust
2	no rust
3	no rust
4	no rust

Results summary

Test tube 1: In test tube 1, the nail is in contact with air and water. It is useful to compare the results in test tubes 2, 3 and 4 with test tube 1 to decide if more or less rusting is taking place. Test tube 1 is called the **control**.

Test tube 2: If you compare test tube 2 with test tube 1 you can see that water is needed for rusting to take place.

Test tube 3: If you compare test tube 3 with test tube 1 you can see that air is needed for rusting to occur.

Test tube 4: Test tube 4 supports this conclusion as no rusting has taken place on this nail that is out of contact with both air and water.

You can conclude from this whole experiment that water and air are both necessary for the steel to rust.

Did You Know?

Aluminium is a more reactive metal than iron but it does not corrode. This is because a very tough aluminium oxide layer forms over the aluminium preventing oxygen and water coming into contact with the aluminium.

Potassium and sodium are very reactive metals. They are stored under oil to prevent them corroding.

---

1. Many millions of pounds are spent every year trying to reduce rusting of iron and steel. Make a list of as many ways of reducing rusting as you can. For each one try to decide why the method works.

2. Stainless steel contains other metals such as nickel and manganese. What is stainless steel used for? What is the advantage of stainless steel over ordinary steel?

3. Steel rusts faster in contact with salty water. The legs of a pier are always under sea water. How do engineers stop the legs from rusting?

8.06 Getting metals from rocks

The photograph on the left shows some children trying to find gold, sieving the tiny stones in a fast-flowing river. This is called panning for gold. They are hoping to find tiny fragments of gold washed down the river from gold deposits in the mountains. They have to sieve a lot of gravel to find a fragment of gold.

Very few materials exist in the Earth as uncombined metals. Only very unreactive metals like gold, platinum and silver can be found as metals.

Usually metals exist in the Earth combined with other elements. Iron, for example, is found either combined with oxygen in an oxide or with sulphur in a sulphide. Sodium is found as sodium chloride and zinc as zinc sulphide.

Ores

An **ore** is a rock which contains a metal or a compound of a metal along with other materials. Iron ore, for example, consists of sandstone rock mixed with iron oxide. An ore is the raw material from which a metal is extracted.

Bauxite is the ore of aluminium. It contains aluminium oxide which is used to produce aluminium. The photograph above shows bauxite being extracted from the Earth by **open-cast mining**.

In *Finding out: Lead from lead oxide* you can make some tiny beads of lead from lead oxide. Lead oxide is made from lead ore.

Did You Know?

Gold can be found in sea water. One cubic mile of sea water contains £100 000 000 worth of gold dissolved in it. However, it is impossible to extract economically because the dissolved gold compounds are mixed with 150 000 000 tonnes of other mineral salts.

---

1. Why do people spend so much time and effort trying to find a few fragments of gold?
2. What are the metals sodium and zinc found combined with in the Earth?
3. Why can bauxite be mined by open-cast mining?
4. Nearly every handful of soil contains aluminium oxide. Why is soil not used as a raw material for aluminium?

Finding out: Lead from lead oxide

We are going to copy the way that people, thousands of years ago, were able to get the metal lead out of rocks. Lead oxide has been made by roasting lead ore in air. When a mixture of this lead oxide and charcoal (carbon) are heated, a reaction takes place. This can be summarized by the word equation:

lead oxide + carbon → lead + carbon dioxide

Instructions

1. Put one spatula measure of lead oxide and one spatula measure of charcoal on the piece of Kaowool paper. With the spatula, mix the two powders thoroughly.

2. Put the Kaowool paper on the support and gauze with the powder spread out over the surface of the paper.

3. Heat the paper strongly. The Kaowool paper does not burn.

4. You should see tiny silvery beads of lead formed. At this stage stop heating.

5. If you can get a tiny bead of lead, you will find it writes on paper like a pencil. Pencils do not contain lead even if we call them lead pencils. They have leads made of mixtures of graphite and clay.

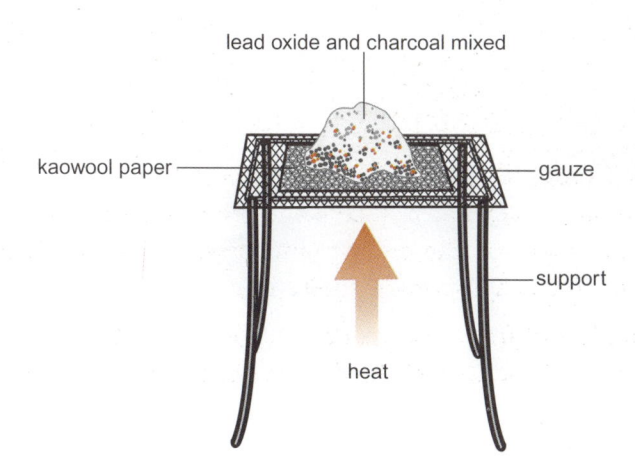

> **WARNING**
>
> Lead compounds are poisonous. Make sure you wash your hands thoroughly after this experiment.

6. Lead was found thousands of years ago when rocks containing lead were heated on charcoal fires. Suggest one advantage and one disadvantage of lead.

8.07 Recycling metals

When will metals run out?

Stocks of some metals are running out. Every year we produce more and more metal objects to make our lives easier. We are using up the valuable stocks of metal ores. The diagram on the left gives some estimates of how long metals will last assuming we carry on using metals as we do now.

We can make metals last longer in various ways. One way is to re-use metals we have used already. We call this **recycling**. At present we recycle metals such as aluminium, lead, tin, copper, silver, and gold.

Household refuse provides a good source of metals for recycling. The diagram shows a new method for separating metals from household refuse. The lumps of metal are arranged on a conveyor belt. The pieces of metal are scanned with X-rays. The different metals then give out X-rays at different frequencies. A microprocessor can look at these X-rays and identify which metal they came from. A swinging arm or a blast of air can be used to separate these metals into different containers. The system can separate five pieces of metal each second. Before this method was developed metals had to be identified visually and picked out by hand.

Length of supply of metals in the Earth

Stages in metal extraction:
1 x-ray detector identifies metal
2 computer relays instructions to air jets
3 air jets blow metal into appropiate bin

Did You Know?

It is estimated that in Great Britain 41 million tonnes of rubbish is burned or dumped each year. If these materials were all recycled they could be worth £1 000 000 000.

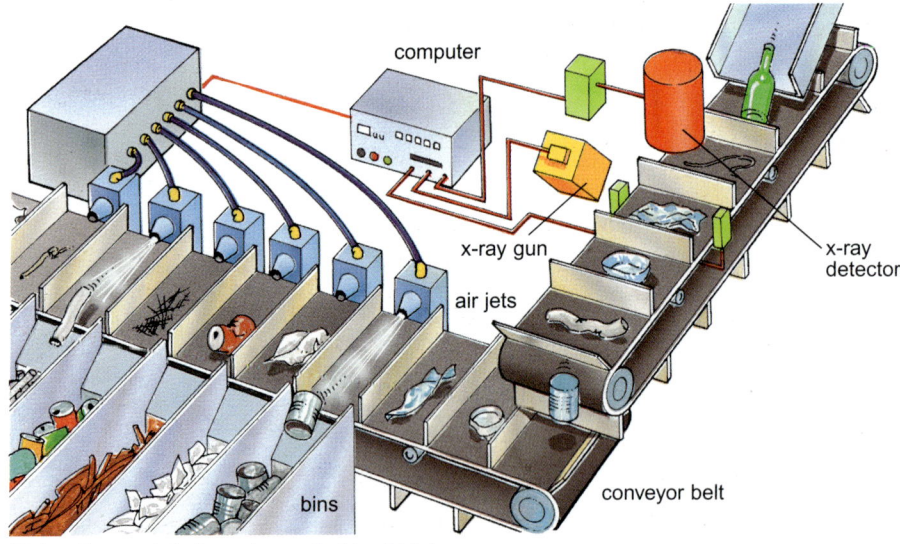

Extracting metals from household rubbish

1. Which metals are likely to be used up first?
2. Which two metals should last longest?
3. Apart from recycling, how could we make metals last longer?
4. Are there any can collection schemes in **a** your school or **b** your community?
5. Cans are made of aluminium or steel. Aluminium cans are more valuable than steel cans. They need to be separated for recycling. How can you tell the difference between a steel can and an aluminium one?

Magnets

CHAPTER 9

9.01

MAGNETISM

Magnets come in all shapes and sizes. There are horseshoe magnets, slab magnets, bar magnets, and ring magnets. All magnets have some parts that show stronger magnetism than others. The strongest parts of a magnet are called its **poles**.

The darkly shaded areas of the magnets are the strongest part – the magnetic poles

Did You Know?

Loudspeakers contain strong magnets. You should never place a recorded tape cassette or a magnetic computer disc near a loudspeaker – it can ruin it.

The poles of bar magnets are near the ends. Those of horseshoe magnets face each other. Slab magnets have poles on the faces and ring magnets have poles on the inner and outer sides.

Magnetic materials

Few materials are strongly **magnetic.** Iron, steel, and nickel are the most common magnetic materials. (Examples of non-magnetic materials include copper, aluminium, wood, and glass.) If you test 'copper' coins you find that those made since 1992 are magnetic. This is because they are in fact made from steel that has been covered, or plated with a layer of copper.

Steel is a useful material for making permanent magnets. Once it has been magnetized it keeps its magnetism for a long time. A piece of steel can be permanently magnetized by placing it inside a coil of wire connected to a battery. The connection is only left for some time.

Iron can be (temporarily) magnetised in this way but loses its magnetism when the battery is disconnected.

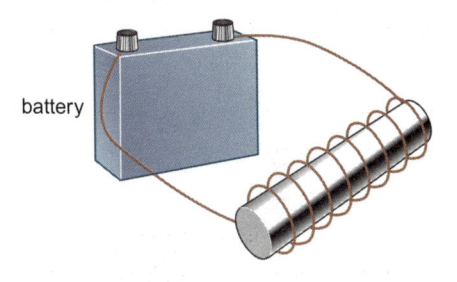

Making a steel bar into a magnet

Magnetic attraction

Paper clips and drawing pins are attracted to magnets. Magnets are also attracted to paper clips and drawing pins and other objects. The diagram on the right shows the attractive force between a magnet and an iron nail. The magnet is attracted to the nail and the nail is attracted to the magnet.

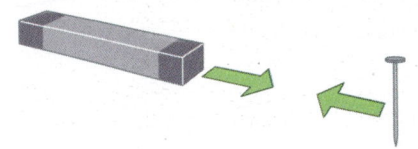

The nail pulls the magnet, the magnet pulls the nail

---

1 Which of these is attracted to a magnet?

copper wire   plastic ruler   iron nail
paper   steel pin   brass button

2 How many other examples of magnetism can you think of?

3 How could you use paperclips to test two magnets to find out which is the stronger?

Draw a diagram to show what you would do and describe how you would tell which one is stronger.

4 If you about to buy an old car. Why might you take a magnet with you?

109

9.02 A magnetic compass

Using a natural compass

For centuries people all over the world have navigated using the stars to guide them. Over each half of the globe there is a **pole star.** This is a very bright star that points the way to the pole. However, stars are not much use during the day or on cloudy nights. Around two thousand years ago the Chinese discovered a new navigational aid. This was a rock called **lodestone.** When it was held so that it could turn freely it always pointed towards the pole. This rock could be easily used by sailors to find their way when travelling during the day as well as on cloudy nights.

A piece of magnetic rock called lodestone

Making a compass

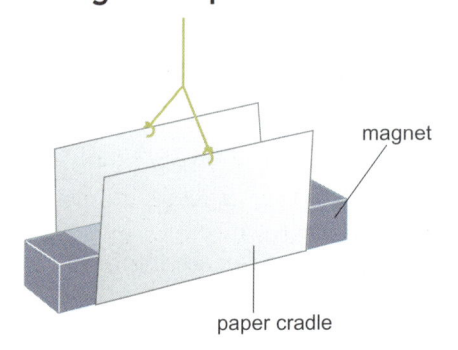

The end of this compass which points to the North Magnetic Pole has a white spot.

The diagram above shows how string and paper can be used to make a cradle for a magnet. If the magnet is placed in the cradle and hung from a piece of string one end points towards the Earth's North Magnetic Pole. If you try this, keep the magnet well away from any magnetic material such as iron or steel.

The end of the magnet that points towards the Earth's North Magnetic Pole is called the north-seeking or north pole of the magnet. This opposite end is the south-seeking or south pole of the magnet. A compass that you buy in a shop is a small magnet that is placed on a needle so that it is free to turn around. The north-seeking pole of a compass needle may be coloured, usually red or blue. But it is always marked. Sometimes it is shaped like an arrow.

The north-seeking pole points towards the Earth's North Magnetic Pole.

The south-seeking pole points towards the Earth's South Magnetic Pole.

Did You Know?

Ships and aircraft no longer need to rely on compasses for navigation. Using navigation satellites, they can pinpoint their position to within ten metres.

1. a Which part of a magnet points towards the Earth's North Magnetic Pole?
   b Which part of a magnet points towards the Earth's South Magnetic Pole?
2. Explain why navigation is easier when using a compass than when relying on the pole star.
3. When using a compass it must be kept away from magnetic materials such as iron and steel. Explain why the compass may not point towards magnetic north if there are other magnetic materials nearby.

Magnetic forces

9.03

There is an **attractive force** between a magnet and a piece of magnetic material such as iron or steel. A magnet pulls an iron paper clip and the paper clip pulls the magnet. Forces act between a magnet and a magnetic object such as a paper clip (iron); each one pulls the other. The paper clip pulls the magnet with the same size force as the magnet pulls the paper clip. There is one important difference: they pull in opposite directions.

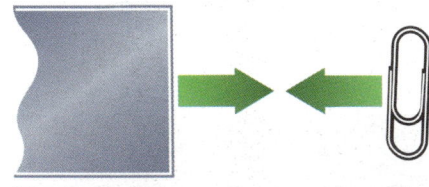

The forces between the magnet and the paper clip are equal in size and they act in opposite directions

Forces between magnets

Magnets can pull other magnets but they can also push them. Whether two magnets pull together or push apart depends on which poles are facing each other.

The diagrams on the right show the forces between pairs of magnets. Two magnets pulling together are **attracting** each other. A pair of magnets pushing apart are **repelling** each other.

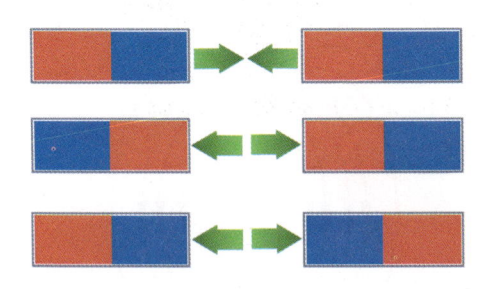

There is a rule for telling whether magnets will attract or repel. If two north-seeking or two south-seeking poles are facing, they repel each other. If a north-seeking pole faces a south-seeking pole, they attract each other. This is summarized in the statement **similar poles repel and opposite poles attract**.

Forces at a Distance

Like gravitational forces, the forces between magnets act at a distance. Magnets do not need to touch each other to be able to push and pull. They even push and pull if they are separated by non-magnetic materials such as paper or plastic.

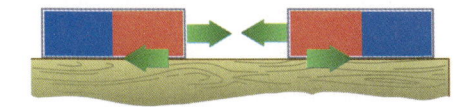

Two magnets placed a distance apart on a table top may not appear to be pulling or pushing each other, but they are. They stay in place because the magnetic forces are not big enough to overcome the friction forces that oppose sliding. The forces between the magnets are strongest when they are at their closest and become weaker when the magnets are pulled further apart.

friction forces prevent these two magnets from moving together

Friction between the magnet and the table

---

1. A child has two toy boats. One has a magnet on top of it, the other has a piece of iron on top of it.

   a Which of the boats could be pulled along with a magnet? Explain why.

   b Which of the boats could be pushed with a magnet? Explain why.

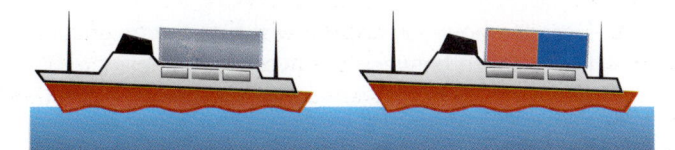

2. How could you use a compass to tell if a piece of steel is magnetized?

   Explain how the results of your experiments would tell you whether the steel is magnetized or not.

3. When using a compass to find your way, it is important to keep it away from any steel object such as a food can (tin-plated steel). Explain such a can could cause the compass to give the wrong information.

111

9.04 Magnetic fields

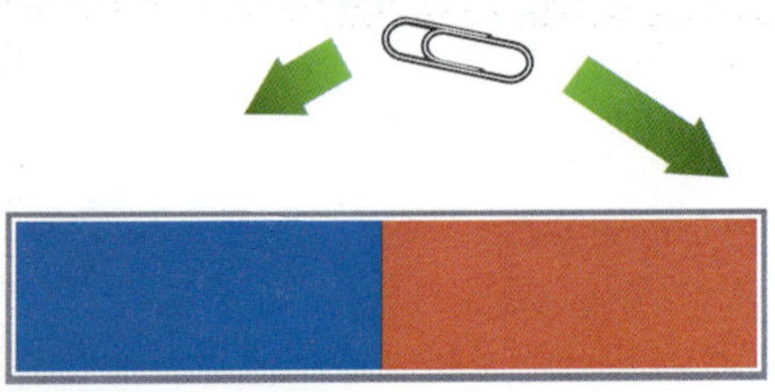

Both poles pull the paper clip, but the nearer pole pulls with the bigger force

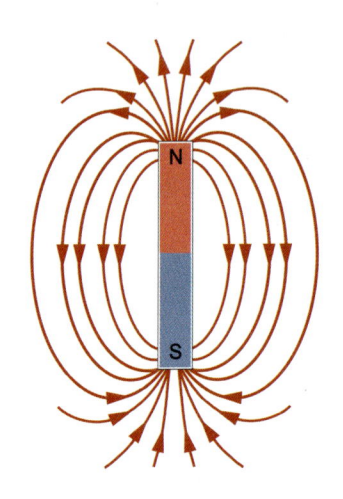

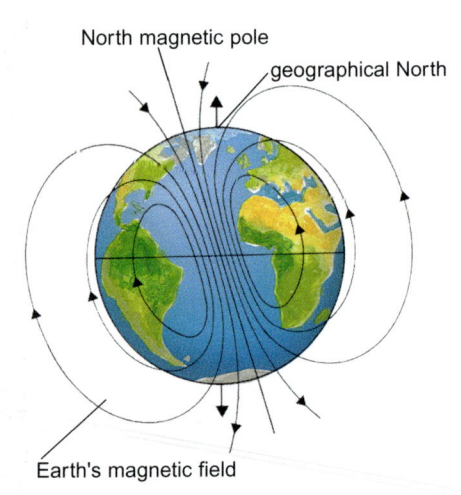

Earth's magnetic field

What is a field?
Magnets can exert forces on other magnets and magnetic materials near to them. Every magnet has its own **magnetic field**. This is the area around a magnet where it can pull and push other magnetic objects. The idea of a magnetic field helps us to explain the forces due to magnetism. A magnet always has its magnetic field around it but it can only exert forces when something magnetic is placed in the field.

The field pattern
If you place a paper clip or drawing pin in a magnetic field you can measure the force that acts on it. This force has a size, measured in newtons, and a direction, shown by an arrow on the diagram. The direction of the force on a paper clip depends on its position in the magnetic field. It is attracted to both poles so it has forces pulling it in two directions at once, rather like a tug-of-war. The nearer pole exerts the bigger force, so it wins and pulls the paper clip towards it.

Magnetic field patterns show the direction of the forces around a magnet. The diagram on the left shows the magnetic field around a bar magnet. Although the field pattern is made up of curved lines, the force at any point acts in a straight line. It just changes direction when you change position.

Arrows on magnetic field lines always point away from a magnet's north-seeking pole and towards its south-seeking pole.

The Earth's magnetic field
The Earth's core is thought to contain a lot of iron that causes its magnetic field. Compasses rely on the Earth's magnetism to be able to point North and South. Although the Earth's North Magnetic Pole is about 700 miles from the geographic North Pole, it is close enough to make little difference. But for precise navigation using a compass, allowance has to be made for the difference positions of the North Pole and the North Magnetic Pole.

While the geographic North Pole always stays in the same place, the North Magnetic Pole is continually moving, at about 10 km/year.

---

1. Describe how you can use a small compass to investigate the direction of the magnetic forces around a magnet.

2. Explain why the north-seeking pole of a compass points towards the Earth's North Pole but away from the north-seeking pole of a magnet.

3. Two bar magnets are placed on a desk with their north poles facing each other.
   a. Describe how you could investigate the magnetic field pattern between the two north poles.
   b. Sketch the results that you would expect to obtain.

Finding out: Magnetic fields

Which way does a compass needle point when it is near a bar magnet? The direction depends on the magnetic field.

Instructions

1 Find out which end of your plotting compass is the north-seeking pole.

2 With a bar magnet in the centre of a large piece of plain paper, place the compass between the magnet and the edge of the paper.

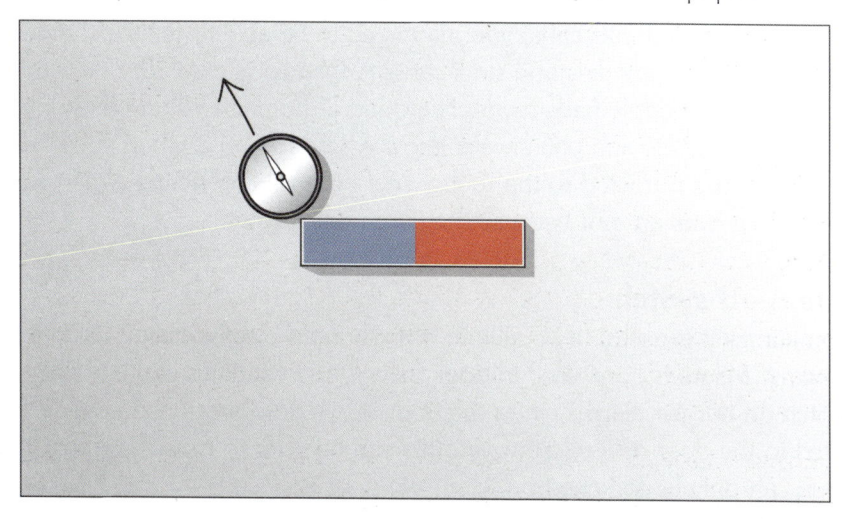

Use a pencil to mark an arrow to show which way the compass is pointing.

3 Move the compass in the direction of your pencil arrow and draw another arrow in the same direction as the compass needle. Keep on doing this until you reach either the magnet or the edge of the paper.

4 Keep on doing this until you have built up a pattern that shows the magnetic field around the magnet.

5 Put the magnet underneath the paper.
Gently sprinkle some iron filings on top of the paper.
Tap the paper – do you see the same pattern as before?

9.05 Using magnets

Magnets have many everyday uses. They can be used to sort iron and steel from other metals, keep doors closed and operate electronic circuits. A magnet made from steel keeps its magnetism for many years, so it can be used to do a job over and over again.

The fridge door

Refrigerators need to be air-tight to keep the cold air in and the warm air out. The door needs to shut firmly and to prevent air moving in and out. The rubber seal fitted to a refrigerator door contains a magnetic strip. This is attracted to the steel casing of the refrigerator, keeping the door tightly shut.

If you recycle drinks cans, you may need to be able to tell the difference between aluminium cans and steel cans. A magnet is used for doing this job, but not many people have magnets around at home. The refrigerator door works just as well, and you always know where to find it when you need it. Steel cans are attracted to the rubber seal because it contains a magnet, but aluminium cans are not because they are non-magnetic.

The reed switch

Sometimes it is useful to be able to switch on an electric circuit using a magnet. Magnets concealed in door frames and windows can be used to switch on burglar alarms when the door or window is opened. A magnet fitted to the door of a microwave oven can be used to make sure that the oven can only be switched on when the door is closed.

A **reed switch** is operated by a magnet. It has two contacts made out of iron. When a magnet is held near to the switch the contacts become magnetized and attract each other. Take the magnet away and they spring apart again. When the switch is used in a circuit, the circuit is only switched on when there is a magnet close by.

This foundry worker is using a magnet to find out which scrap objects contain iron

Magnetic board games are useful in cars

The reed switch contacts are normally apart. They come together when a magnet is held nearby

---

1. Describe how you could use the door of a refrigerator to sort out some empty drinks cans into two groups, cans that are made out of iron and cans that are made out of aluminium.

2. Draw a diagram of a circuit that uses a reed switch to turn a light on and off.

3. Some cat owners have cat flaps fitted to an outside door. The flap opens to allow the cat in and out of the house. How could you use a magnet, an electrically-operated lock and a reed switch so that the flap can only open when the cat is near to it?

4. Look around your home. How many uses for magnets can you find?

Induced magnetism

9.06

Magnetic induction

If you hold an iron can or other iron object near to a magnet the can itself becomes magnetized. This is called **induced magnetism**; it only lasts while the iron can is near the magnet. Induced magnetism is used to explain why iron cans and other iron objects such as paper clips are attracted to fixed magnets.

When a magnet picks up a paper clip it makes the paper clip into a **temporary magnet**. If the north-seeking pole of the magnet is used, the part of the paper clip touching the magnet becomes a south-seeking pole.

Because the paper clip is now a magnet, it will attract other paper clips and objects made from magnetic materials. The diagram shows the induced magnetic poles when paper clips are suspended from a magnet and when a pair of scissors is attracted to a strong horseshoe magnet.

Induced poles (in a pair of scissors)

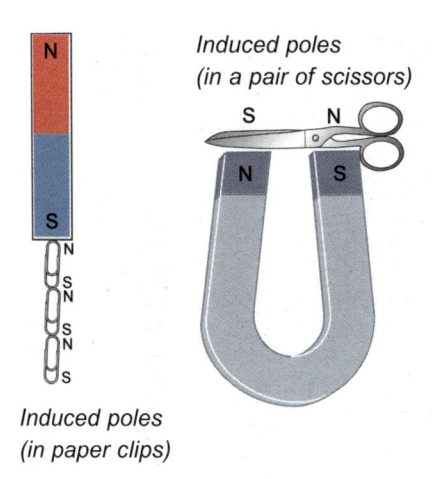

Induced poles (in paper clips)

How does induction work?

A piece of unmagnetized iron has lots of regions, called **domains**, that are magnetized. When these domains are arranged randomly, without any ordering, they cancel out each other's magnetism. The domains are sensitive to magnetic fields. If a magnet is placed nearby its magnetic field causes the domains to line up in an orderly way. This makes the iron into a magnet. With the magnetic field from all the domains acting in the same direction they no longer cancel out but reinforce each other.

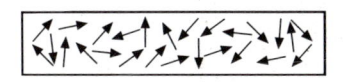

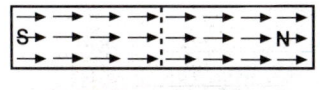

The domains in unmagnetized iron (top) line up in an orderly way when a magnet is nearby (bottom)

Using iron and steel

Iron is a 'soft' magnetic material, it is easy to magnetize by induction. It also loses its magnetism easily. The domains return to their random ordering when the magnet is taken away.

Steel is a 'hard' magnetic material. It is more difficult to align the domains in a piece of unmagnetized steel than it is in a piece of unmagnetized iron. However, once they are aligned they stay in an orderly arrangement.

Steel ships become magnetized when they are being built. The repeated hammering of rivets to join the steel plates together disturbs the domains. They align themselves with the Earth's magnetic field so that the finished ship is like a large permanent magnet.

Did You Know?

Video tapes record television programmes using magnetism. Cassette tapes record music and speech. When you record a programme, the information is stored as a pattern of magnetic domains on the tape.

---

1. Use a diagram to explain how the domains in the pair of scissors shown in the top diagram become aligned when it is attracted to the horseshoe magnet.
2. How could you use a small compass to show that paper clips suspended from a permanent magnet have two opposite magnetic poles?
3. Explain why steel is used, rather than iron, to make permanent magnets.

115

Index

acceleration 78
acid 36
  strength 38
active movement 8
adaptation 17
adolescence 95
air resistance 81
algae 59
alkali 36
  strength 38
alloy 104
ammeter 45
amoeba 17
ampere 45
amphibian 60
animal phyla 60
animal 58
anther 92
antibody 99
arthropod 60
asexual reproduction 89
attraction 53
attractive force 53, 111

baby 99
bacteria 17
battery 43, 46
bird 60
blastula 99
boiling 22, 66, 67
  point 22, 69
breast 97
burning 32, 33, 103

carbonate 39
reaction with acid 39
cell 10, 11, 13, 14, 17, 43, 46
  animal 13, 15
  plant
cell wall 14
cellulose 14
changes in boys and girls 95
chemical changes 41
chemical reaction 31
chlorophyll 14
chloroplast 14, 17
chordate 60
chromatogram 72
chromatography 71, 72, 73
circuit 44, 47, 48, 49, 50, 51, 52
  diagram 43, 46, 47
class 61
classification 54, 57
colloid 30
combustion 32, 33
component 43
condensation 25, 66, 67
condenser 67

condensing 66, 67
conductivity 103
conductor 42, 100
cooling 25
corrosion 105
crystal 27
  making 28, 29
current 46, 48, 49
  in parallel circuits 49, 51, 52
  in series circuits 47, 51
  measuring, 45
cytoplasm 13, 14

deceleration 79
digestive system 19
discovery of oxygen 34
dissolving 26
distillation 66, 67, 68, 69
DNA 10, 13
domain 115
dormancy 93
driving force 75, 78, 81
ductile 103

Earth 80, 81
  gravitation 80, 81, 83, 84, 88
  pull of the 80, 81, 83, 84, 85, 88
effervescence 102
egg 98
ejaculation 96
elastic 86, 88
electric charge 53
electric current 45
electrical conductivity 101
electricity 42-52
electron microscope 14
embryo 99
erection 96
ethanol 68, 69
evaporation 23, 65
evolution 57, 58, 60
excretion 9
extraction of metal 106, 107

falling 82
fallopian tube 97, 98
families 61
fermentation 70
fern 59
fertilization 89, 90, 93, 95, 98
filament 46, 49, 52
filtration 65
fish 60
floating 84
flower reproduction 92
flower structure 91
flower 90
foetus 99

follicle 97
force (s) 74, 75, 80, 82, 83, 87
  balanced 79, 84
  downward 83, 85, 84
  gravitational 80, 81
  measuring 74
  stretching 86
  unbalanced 78, 81, 85
  upward 83, 84, 85
fractional distillation 68, 69
free-fall motion 81
freeze 25
freezing point 25
friction 75, 77
fuel 32
fungi 58

gamete 95
gas 22
genera 61
genus 61
germinate 93
gravitational force 80, 81
growth 9
gut 19

heart 18
heating 24
heating substances, 40
hormone 98
human life cycle 95
human reproduction 95, 96, 97

ice 25
immiscible liquid 68
indicator 36, 103
insoluble 26
insulator 42
intercourse 97, 98
isomorphous 27

jellyfish 60

key 62
kingdom 58, 61

lamp 43
leaf 20
lens 11
life 10
life processes 8
Light Emitting Diode (LED) 47
liquid 22
litmus 36
lodestone 110

magnet 44, 100, 109, 110, 111, 112, 114
  making a 109

magnetic attraction **109, 111, 114**
  compass **110**
  field **112, 113, 115**
  forces **80, 111**
  induction **115**
  material **109**
  pole, **110**
  repulsion **111**
magnetism **109, 110, 111, 112, 114**
  induced **115**
  permanent **109**
  temporary **109**
mains electricity **42**
malleable **103**
mammal **60**
mass **33**
melting **22**
melting point **22**
membrane **13, 14**
menstrual cycle **98**
metal **42, 100, 101, 102, 103, 104, 105**
  extraction **106, 107**
  ore, **106**
  properties of **103**
  reaction with acid **101, 102**
  reaction with air/oxygen **102**
micropyle **93**
microscope **11, 12**
  compound **11**
  electron **14**
  simple **11**
miscible liquid **68, 69**
mollusc **60**
moss **59**
movement **9**
muscle **18**

nectar **92**
negative **46**
nervous system **19**
neutral **36**
newton **72**
non-metal **101**
nucleic acid **10**
nucleus **13, 14**
nutrition **9**

open-cast mining **106**
order **61**
ore **106**
organ **18, 21**
ovary **93, 97**
oviduct **97**
ovule **93**
oxidation **102, 103**
oxide **102, 105, 106, 107**
oxygen **32**

palisade tissue **18**
parallel circuit **44, 49, 50, 51**
passive movement **8**
penis **96, 98**
period **98**
ph **38**
  scale **38, 103**
phloem **20**
phlogiston theory **35**
phyla **59, 61**
physical changes **41**
placenta **99**
plant **58, 92**
  cell **13, 16**
  phyla **59, 61**
plastic **86, 88**
polarity **111**
pole **109, 111, 112**
pollen **92, 93, 94**
  grain **94**
  tube **94**
pollination **92**
positive terminal **46**
protist **17, 58**
puberty **95**
pulling **74**
pure substances **63**
purification of rock salt **65**
pushing **74**

reaction **101, 102**
recycling metal, **108**
red cabbage **37**
reed switch **44, 114**
refining crude oil **70**
reproduction **9, 89, 95**
reproductive system **19, 97**
reptile **60**
repulsion **53, 111**
resistance **44**
resistive force **77, 78, 81**
resistor **51**
respiration **9**
responsive system **19**
RNA **10**
rock salt **64**
roots **20**
rust **105**

secondary sex
  characteristics **95**
seed formation **93**
seed plant **59, 90**
segmented worm **60**
semen **96, 98**
sensitivity **9**
separating mixtures **63**
series **44, 46, 48, 51, 52**

  circuit **44, 48, 50**
sexual reproduction **89**
sinking **83**
skin **18**
solid **22**
soluble **26**
solute **26**
solution **26**
  saturated, **26**
solvent **26**
specialist cell **18**
specialized cell **17**
species **57, 61**
speed **76, 78, 81**
  changing, **78**
  constant, **79, 81**
sperm **96, 98**
spore **59**
spring **87, 88**
stamen **94**
state change of, **22**
stigma **92, 93, 94**
stomata **20**
style **93, 94**
suspension **30**
switch **43, 44**
symbol **43**
system **19, 20, 21**

terminal velocity **81**
testicle (teste) **96**
theory of combustion **35**
tissue **18**
transformer **48**
transport system **20**

universal indicator **38**
uses of fractional distillation **70**

vacuole **14**
vagina **97, 98**
vapour **22**
variation **54, 55, 56**
  continuous **55**
  discontinuous **55**
virus **10**
voltage **46, 52**
von Linné (or Linnaeus) **61**

water **68, 69**
weight **83**
whisky making **70, 97**
womb **98**
word equation **102**

xylem **18, 20**

zygote **95, 99**